William Horton

LIVING ON

BORROWED

TIME

AUTHOR
William Horton

TRANSCRIBED BY
Kathy Rose

EDITED BY
Chelsea Heath

DESIGNED BY
Jonah Rose

For more images and letters

visit www.WilliamHorton.net

WILLIAM HORTON

Living On

BORROWED

TIME

FOREWORD

Ever since I can remember my Dad has been telling his World War II stories. His memory is incredible. Over and over people have said, "Someone needs to get these down."

When I retired, I decided to give it a shot. I went over to my Dad's once a week for about a year. He would talk while I typed the stories. I recorded them exactly as he told them to me.

Typing is not my area of expertise, so the book needed a lot of editing. That's where my niece Chelsea Heath came in. She spent many hours editing, sometimes calling Dad to confirm or rephrase facts. We are forever grateful for the time she spent.

Once the editing was complete came the layout, cover and publishing. That's where my son Jonah Rose came in. I want to thank him for his tremendous help.

My nephew Nathan Heath helped with publishing and created a website at www.williamhorton.net to share more letters and full quality photos. I appreciate his contribution very much.

This book was a labor of love and we hope you will enjoy it!

-Kathy Horton-Rose

INTRODUCTION
In the Beginning

After I got back from serving combat in the Army for 21 months in World War II, I told my mom I thought I was living on borrowed time. She said I was living on borrowed time a lot longer than that.

My twin sister and I were born premature in 1925 in Hanston, Kansas. We weighed four pounds apiece. My mother was very sick and running a high fever. When the doctor got there he said he thought he could save my mother, but not my sister and I, so my grandmother took over.

There was a blizzard outside and it was difficult to heat the house. To keep us warm, Grandma opened the oven and put us in a shoebox on the oven door. By nighttime when the oven fire was burning low, Grandma decided to put us in bed with my mother, who was still hot from her fever. She watched over us all night. By the next morning we were all feeling better.

We moved to Jetmore, Kansas when I was six years old and I started school. Even though our family was poor, we kids had a happy childhood. When I wasn't in school, I spent most of my time catching frogs, swimming in the creek, roller skating, and celebrating all our holidays with big chicken dinners at our Grandma Abbott's.

We moved to Portland in 1942 when I was 17 years old. We came out to Oregon in an open pickup. There were three adults in the front, and in the back there were four kids, two dogs and all of our belongings. As we passed through Denver, Colorado it was snowing, but when we got to Oregon it was raining mildly.

I started at Franklin High School in September of 1942. Franklin had 1,500 new students, a lot of them from families that came out to Oregon to work in the shipyards. I got out of school in June of 1943 and went right into the army. I had just finished my junior year of high school, so I didn't graduate before being drafted, but I got my diploma after I returned.

CHAPTER 1
How I Got Into the Army

How did I get into the Army? Did I volunteer? No. Was I drafted? No. My friends and neighbors selected me. This was what the draft papers said anyway. I turned 18 in January of 1943. Soon after that I received notice to report for my physical to be classified. I got out of school in June and received another notice to report for another physical. They checked my eyes to see if I was colorblind, they checked my ears, and they sent me from one room to another to get various parts checked.

In the last room, they asked me to raise my right hand and repeat after them. Then I was asked if I wanted to be in the Army, Navy or Marines. I don't know why, but I chose the Army. I was told to report at the train station on August 7th to go to Fort Lewis in Washington State. The first thing they did when we got on the train was feed us, and I knew right then I wasn't going to like the Army because they gave us green beans.

While at Fort Lewis, we were issued clothing and shoes. I think that's where the phrase "one size fits all" comes from. If a soldier were extra big or small, getting clothes or shoes that fit could be a problem. I noticed one fellow in line getting clothes, and he had been issued a shirt of one kind and trousers of another. He was a big guy, so they didn't match. That's why I learned to always order 32"x32". It was a common size. A little long in the leg for me, but I just tucked the extra into my boots.

Like most army camps, Fort Lewis had a PX (post exchange store) where we could buy just about anything – stationery, candy bars, ice cream. A pint of ice cream was a dime. The first thing we bought was shoe polish. We were issued two pairs of shoes, which were to be polished at all times. We were to wear one pair of shoes one day and the other the next day and so forth. The problem was that I ended up with two pairs of shoes that wore out at the same time. Instead of getting new shoes when ours wore out, they were sent into town and new soles were put onto them.

CHAPTER 2
Basic Training

We stayed at Fort Lewis for a week, and then we got onto a train to Fort McClellan in Alabama for basic training. We were on the train for about 4½ days. Our train got into camp after dark. A bunch of men got onto the train and started giving orders – "do this," "do that," "say, 'yes sir'" or "say, 'no sir'." There were 80 of us from the northwest, and the rest of our group was made up of men from the South.

I spent 16 weeks in Fort McClellan, Alabama learning all the skills needed to be an infantryman. We were housed in buildings called huts. There were 16 men in each building. There were no sheets on the bed, so we took the mattress pads off and used them for sheets. Each man had to sweep the area around his bed and mop the floor each morning. The showers and restrooms were across the street, and the dining area was about two buildings down.

We didn't go anywhere on our own. We had to wait until they blew the whistle, and we were to be lined up out in the street before the sound stopped. Everywhere we went we had to march. We even had to march to the mess hall. We had to carry a rifle everywhere we went as well.

We were paid $50 a month, but had to pay $10 for insurance, and $10 to get our clothes cleaned. We got up at 4am, and sometimes didn't get to bed until after 9pm. We didn't have time to get homesick.

During the 16 weeks of basic training we had to learn a little bit of everything. We learned how to fire a rifle, a machine gun and a bazooka, how to throw a hand grenade, and how to do hand-to-hand combat.

We practiced with the machine guns. The day we were supposed to go out and fire a machine gun for the record, I had a sore finger, so I didn't go. Later I went out with another company and fired the machine gun. They set us up on a 1,000-inch range to shoot targets with 1-inch squares. They were set up on a grid with some across, some down and some diagonal. We couldn't see what we were shooting, but we each had an observer. The object was to get one bullet in each square. If we missed, the observer told us what correction to make. I had a good observer. I ended up getting the highest score of the day.

We also had to do an obstacle course at night where we crawled under barbed wire while shots were going off overhead. Another training skill we learned was how to put on a gas mask. We had to go into a building full of gas, and after we were there a few minutes, we had to take off the mask so we would know what the gas smelled like.

In November, we went out into the field for two weeks of training. It was a 28-mile hike one way, carrying a full field pack. After the first hour we got a 15-minute break, then 10 minutes every hour after that. It took us over 80 hours. We were pretty much wiped out by the time we got there, but we still had to pitch our tents. Boy, were we ready to go to bed! The men from the South, though, didn't even work up a sweat. They built a big bonfire and sang songs. It got pretty cold at night and water froze in our tents.

One night we were ordered to go up onto a hill and set up our tents with no lights and no noise. Two of the men tried to find a lump in their bed with a cigarette lighter. The lighter had leaked some fluid and we could see the light flare up a mile away. They spent the rest of the night sitting up with a machine gun.

Our training ended just before Christmas. We were to report at Fort Meade in 17 days, which gave us time to go home for Christmas before going overseas.

After the holidays, we were transferred to Fort Meade in Maryland, just outside of Washington, D.C. We stayed over in Washington D.C. on January 6th. I remember because that was my 19th birthday. We arrived at about 9pm. We got to see some of the tourist sights. It amazed me how many things we saw in one day. We got first-class treatment, being members of the service.

We checked in at Fort Meade on noon the next day. We were there just a week. From there we went to Camp Patrick Henry near Norfolk, Virginia, then shipped out for overseas. I left Norfolk on January 23rd, 1944 and returned on October 12th, 1945.

CHAPTER 3
Off to War

We left Norfolk, Virginia on the 23rd day of January 1944. We boarded a ship called the William Blunt, a liberty ship built in Portland, Oregon. There were 56 ships in our convoy. It took us 21 days to get overseas because the convoy could only go as fast as the slowest ship. Some days when I went on deck I could see ships everywhere I looked. Other days I couldn't see one ship.

There were 500 troops plus the crew on board. We all slept in the hold. We had two meals a day. To relieve the boredom I played checkers or sat on deck looking for fish. The only fish I ever saw was during a storm when I saw some flying fish. Being from Kansas, I had never seen the ocean before. I was disappointed because I had thought the ocean was full of fish.

They didn't tell us where we were going until several days after we left. Then we found out we were going to Oran, North Africa. We arrived in Oran on the 12th of February. We could see Oran from the harbor, but I never got to go there. I got stuck on baggage detail, so I didn't get to go to camp with the rest of the guys. We had to stay in the harbor until the trucks came to pick up the baggage, which was about four in the morning.

In the U.S. all the windows had to be blocked out and the streetlights turned off at night. Here, the whole dock was lit up.

I asked one of the dockworkers if they weren't afraid of being bombed. He said, "The Germans know where we are, so there's no use trying to hide from them."

We stayed in this camp for four days before leaving for Italy. All I remember is that we had butter made of camel's milk and delicious, red-meat oranges. The butter didn't have much of a taste. I got paid with U.S. money backed by gold. It could be cashed in for gold. I should have kept it, but I sent it home.

The ship we boarded for Italy was a Scottish luxury liner converted to a troop ship and run by the British. All orders were given in French and English. When we were boarding there was a company of North African soldiers. They were a rugged bunch. One had a monkey, one had a big jug of wine, and they all carried big knives.

We slept in hammocks above the tables that we ate on. They were a lot more comfortable than the bunks on our ship. Every morning a British officer would shout, "Rise and shine, you lucky lads, and get your bread and butter!" Most of our meals were soybeans and bread. Being British, they gave us tea five times a day and sold it in between for five cents a cup.

The native troops sat around sharpening their knives. Every time before putting them away, they tested the sharpness by poking themselves until they drew blood. They also had a game they played where they sat in a circle with a piece of paper in the middle. The object of the game was to grab the paper before getting stabbed. I never played that game.

One day they thought there was a submarine following us, so they dropped depth charges overboard. A depth charge is a weapon used to attack submerged submarines. It sounded like someone pounding on the side of the ship with a big hammer. Nothing came of it.

I got to see the Rock of Gibraltar, which is at the tip of southern Spain at the mouth of the Mediterranean. We landed in Italy on the 19th of February.

CHAPTER 4
Italy 1944

When we got off the ship, we got onto a train. It took us to a farm that was used as a replacement center. Mussolini's son owned it. We were there for about four days.

In getting equipped to go to the front I was issued a rifle. I took the rifle to my tent to check it out because I knew it had just come from the front. I took it apart and found that one of the metal pins had been replaced with a matchstick, so I took it back and got another one.

They told us we were going to the front the next day. They took us out into the pouring rain and gave us our paychecks. Maybe they didn't want us to die broke. The next day we went to Naples to take a ship to Anzio. Before we even got on the ship we could hear the rumble of gunfire and see the sky lit up like fireworks.

The ship we were on had 60 truckloads of ammunition on board. German airplanes were following us most of the way, so our anti-aircraft guns were firing constantly.

When we got to the harbor at Anzio the front of the ship opened up and the loaded trucks were driven out. They were driven straight to a more secure area to be unloaded, and the empty trucks were sent back to be loaded again.

We came off the ship and walked right up the main street.

After about two blocks we came to a railway station. I thought we were waiting for a train. We stayed there until it started to get dark, then several big trucks came to pick us up. They took us to an open field and told us to spread out and dig in for the night. My buddy Ivan Hood and I dug a hole big enough for the two of us to sleep in. It was a quiet night.

When we woke up it was a whole different world. There were anti-aircraft guns firing all around us. German artillery shells were going off in the field next to ours. My buddy Ivan stuck his head up and said, "Sometimes I think a dishonorable discharge wouldn't be so bad." Fortunately none of us were hurt.

At about 10am a jeep came up and an officer got out. He had a clipboard with a list of names to be assigned to different units. We were assigned in alphabetical order. Ivan Hood was assigned to the 1st Battalion, but they didn't call my name. When there were 10 men left, we were assigned to the 2nd Medical Battalion as litter bearers. Of the 10 men, I was the only one whose last name did not start with an M or an S. That is how I got into the medics.

CHAPTER 5
I Am Now a Medic

We were taken to the 2nd Battalion aid station. They informed us of our duties and gave us instructions on how to perform them. We were instructed on how to administer blood to a wounded soldier. We were each given a canvas vest with two large pockets. They were filled with bandages and supplies to treat the wounded. On the sides of the vest above the pockets was a strip of heavy canvas that made a loop to stick the stretcher poles in while carrying a wounded man on a litter. Later on I would reflect that I wished I had gotten more training. I felt like I could have helped more if I had known what the heck I was doing. I didn't even know what some of the supplies were for.

We had bandages, morphine and other medical supplies in one of the large pockets, and dried blood plasma in the other. Blood needed to be kept refrigerated, but plasma was easily dried and transported. A soldier's blood type was listed on their dog tag, but we didn't worry about plasma type. We used a lot of plasma. Someone would come in with blue lips looking like he was dead, but as soon as we could get plasma into him, he'd be up smoking a cigarette.

A unit of blood plasma came in two bottles. One contained sterile water and the other dried plasma. The tops of the bottles were sealed with rubber. There was a package of needles and two rubber tubes needed to mix the plasma and use it. One end of the shorter tube had two needles for mixing the dried plasma and the water. There was another piece of tubing about two feet long with a needle on each end. One end went into the mixed plasma and the other end went into the wounded soldier. The bottle was held upside down until all the plasma was distributed.

Next we were told to go out and dig foxholes near the aid station. We dug the holes, covered them with cardboard, and piled all the dirt we had dug out on top. This left just enough room to get underneath, creating a tunnel out of the cardboard, which protected us from what were called "butterfly bombs." Canisters filled with these small bombs were dropped and they would scatter all over.

After about a week they told us we were going up to the front to a secondary position. This is so we would be used to being up at the front before we were actually sent into front-line combat. As we went up to the front it was raining and the sky was lit up with artillery fire. We went up a little road that met a bigger road that was an overpass. Just before we got to the overpass, they told us to hold up because they were shelling the overpass. Even though we weren't there yet, there was shrapnel flying over our heads. This was the first time I had ever been that close to shells going off.

When we got to the overpass, we turned right and were about a mile from where we were going to stay. Since we were replacing another unit we didn't have to dig foxholes, we just took over theirs. The only trouble was, we were one foxhole short. Guess who was left out? My buddy and I found a spot between two foxholes where they had used the dirt to cover their foxholes. There was a hole about 18 inches deep, just enough for us to lie down in with a little protection. We slept that way for 10 nights.

We had only been there about 10 minutes when a German dropped a few mortar shells in our area. One soldier was wounded. We didn't have to go very far to get to him, about 20 feet. As we were putting him on the stretcher, a shell went off and I was hit in the finger with a piece of shrapnel. When we got close to the crossroads, a jeep came to take him back to the aid station. The mud was about knee-deep, so we were pretty worn out when we got back to our makeshift foxhole. He was our only wounded in the 10 days we were there.

As a litter bearer, we were responsible for picking up the wounded, but not the dead. There was a crew called grave registration that took care of the dead. The grave registration guys stayed with us a lot. That's a job I don't think I'd want. If we went to pick up a wounded guy and he had died, and there weren't any other guys alive and wounded, we'd go ahead and take him back.

One morning while we were there, I was just hanging out with some of the guys when we spotted a dogfight between two planes. One was a British Spitfire and the other a German plane. The British plane shot down the German plane and there was a trail of smoke. The German pilot parachuted out and was picked up in another area. It reminded me of a movie I saw about World War I.

Another day there was an American tank disabled on the road. A German plane saw the tank, and not knowing it was disabled, shot a row of bullets right along the side of the road not more than 20 feet from where we were.

CHAPTER 6

The Worst 10 Days of My Life

During the 10 days before Easter in 1944 we were sent up to the front near the Mussolini Canal. Mussolini had planned on building a resort there, so he had canals built to drain off the water. We would be in one canal and the Germans in the next one over. In between was no-man's land.

About a block from the canal was a house. They stored supplies there. Every night they would bring us K-rations (individual daily combat food rations), water, ammunition and any other supplies we needed from the supply depot. It was too dangerous to do during the day.

We got three K-rations that were passed out each night for the following day - one for breakfast, one for lunch and one for supper. They came in a box shaped like a Cracker Jack box, only a little bigger, and made out of real heavy wax paper. The top opened, and we'd take the canteen cup, punch holes in the sides of the box, and light the top of the box to heat a cup of powdered coffee. It didn't smoke much to give away our position. I never drank coffee until I learned to make it myself. Spending all day in a foxhole, we could spend a lot of time making a cup of coffee.

In every ration there were three cigarettes (a total of nine per day), a little deal of toilet paper, and what we called dog biscuits. They gave us a simple can opener, dextrose tablets, and orange powder for an orange drink. For breakfast, there was a package of powdered coffee, and a can of ham and eggs or pork and eggs. For lunch we got a can of cheese (like a can of tuna fish).

Dinner was a different story. Evening meal was a can of corned pork loaf with apple flakes. I've never eaten any dog food, but I think it would probably taste better. I never met anyone who liked it. We also got bouillon powder. Some guys sprinkled it on the pork loaf and burned it black. I hate to think how much pork loaf was thrown away.

We got a D-bar, which was solid chocolate, and pretty good. That's what kept guys going. We got the same thing every day. If we wanted variety, we could eat our lunch ration for breakfast and our breakfast ration for lunch. There were 5-in-1 rations or 10-in-1 rations that were meant for bigger groups of guys and had more variety. Sometimes they'd have canned bacon or pineapple or candy bars. We didn't get C-rations very often, but they'd have canned beans or hash and needed to be heated up.

I didn't smoke but I carried cigarettes and matches everywhere I went. I never got around to smoking them, which was probably one of the smartest things I ever did. It was no problem getting cigarettes. On the front line overseas we got all the cigarettes we wanted. Behind the front lines, they were five cents each. One time I left 10 cartons in a foxhole because no one wanted them.

Our foxholes were dug right along the bank. We never got out of our foxholes unless we had to, because we didn't know when the shells would be coming in. The only time we came out of our holes was to pick up the wounded, or to go to the house for supplies. One night they told us not to go to the house until after 7pm because the Germans were going to shell it at 7pm, and they did!

No matter what time of day a soldier was wounded, we generally had to wait until dark to move them back to the rear. We would bring them to the house to wait for a vehicle to take them back to the aid station.

One day someone stuck their head into our foxhole and told us that the mortar crew had gotten a direct hit. When we got down to the mortar crew, one young soldier was laying there. He was dead, but there wasn't a mark on him. He looked so peaceful, I thought, "If that's what it's like to be dead, it can't be too bad."

One of the other mortar crew was seriously wounded. The aid man had bandaged him up and told us, "He is in serious condition." Ordinarily we would wait until nightfall to take him to the house to be picked up. We didn't know whether he could live that long, so we started taking him right down the center of the canal to get him back to the aid station. We thought if we went down into the canal they wouldn't be able to see us. In some places the water was so deep the four of us bearing the litter had to lift the patient above our heads to keep him out of the water.

It took about five hours. Finally the stream came right behind the house where the aid station was. We took him inside and the medical officer said, "It's a good thing you brought him in now. He might not have lasted until nightfall." It made us feel good that someone might live because we got him back in time. We were tired, so they let us stay there for the night, but we had to go back before daylight.

The 2nd Platoon was close enough to the Germans that they could throw hand grenades at them. Most of the fighting was done during the day, but this time there was a battle happening with shells and grenades and rifle fire all going off in the middle of the night. It was about midnight when we got called up to get a man who had appendicitis.

As we went up the ditch we had to bend over, and it was hard to walk because the ditch had about two feet of mud in it. We got him on the stretcher but had a heck of a time carrying him back through all the mud. By the time we got him back to the main canal, he was covered in mud. We washed him off and took him the rest of the way to the house where he could be picked up. We heard later that they had operated on him and he was fine. That was probably not the best place to have an attack of appendicitis.

Between the Germans and the Americans was a plain of flat land. Some of our soldiers had foxholes there. They didn't dare come out during the day. If they had to relieve themselves they used a K-ration box.

We waited until nighttime to go pick up a soldier who was wounded in one of the foxholes. He had been shot. The bullet had gone in one cheek and out the other. It wasn't a vital wound, but very painful. Just as we got to the foxhole the Germans started shelling. I got hit. The top of my knee was grazed and there was a groove about ¼-inch deep. There was a hole in my pants that went in one side and out the other. That's how I got one of my three Purple Hearts.

One morning we got a call that a man was wounded in the 1st Battalion. He had a foxhole dug in the bank just big enough for him, but his feet stuck out. A mortar shell landed right between his feet. When we got there the aid man assigned to that battalion had bandaged him up. The soldier looked down at his feet and said, "I'll probably lose my feet, but I'm still alive."

About a quarter of a mile down from our foxhole the canal turned. Up on the bank was a house the Germans shelled from time to time. They probably thought we were using it for observation. My foxhole buddy and I each had half of a tent. We used one half to cover up the bottom of the hole to sleep on, and draped the other half on top to keep the rain out. Sometimes the shells would miss the house and land in the canal, and the shrapnel would hit the half of the tent we had over the entrance to our shelter. In 10 days we had 17 holes in the tent. We also had 10 shells that went off within 10 feet of our foxhole.

Finally we got called back to the rear and another outfit came to take our place. There was no safe place, but we were in a safer spot. The following day was Easter. I had left home on the 2nd of January, and the first mail from home I received was on Easter morning. I got 17 letters, most from my twin sister Betty. It was really good to finally hear from home. We didn't get a lot of mail because it had to catch up to us.

CHAPTER 7

Life on the Beachhead

Most of the time we moved from one position to the other, replacing men on the front line and men in reserve. My litter squad was attached to Company F. Where they went, we went, too. There were four men in our squad. We were separated into groups of two. Bob Maxon was my buddy. CJ and Charlie were buddies with one another. Coincidentally, Bob and I were from the Northwest and CJ and Charlie were from down South.

One day Bob and I heard that some of our buddies we had trained with were nearby. Shortly after that, we got PX rations that were considered luxury items – cigars and a couple cans of beer and Coke. I traded my beer for Coke, and since I didn't smoke cigars, I decided to take them over to Johnson, who I had met in basic training. I knew he smoked cigars.

There were five of them there and I had taken basic training with all of them. We enjoyed talking to each other and comparing experiences. While we were talking, one of the guys said, "The next time we get together, there will probably be some of us missing." By the next month, four of the five men had been killed.

There was a large area of pine trees on the beach we called "The Pines." It was a quiet area, and if we got a few days off we were moved there. Everybody dug a foxhole and put a shelter halfway over the top, which was the same color as the sand. Oftentimes at night when it was dark, guys would fall into foxholes and sometimes there might already be someone in them. Putting down white tape to guide the soldiers at night solved this problem.

We also had a tent set up to show movies. The sides of the tent were sandbagged. We didn't have any chairs so we had to sit on our helmets. Sometimes during the movie we could feel the ground shaking from shells going off in the vicinity.

We spent the next couple of months waiting around to push off for Rome. One day several of us were in a ravine so the Germans couldn't see us. We had our mess kits out and were having breakfast when we heard, "BOOM, swish, swish, swish." A German plane had dropped its bomb to get rid of the weight because three British Spitfires were right on its trail. It happened so fast we didn't realize what was going on. Mess kits were flying everywhere and it took quite a while to pick everything up afterwards.

Another place we spent time waiting was right along a small stream. There were already foxholes dug straight into the bank. Ants occupied the hole that Bob and I were in. They didn't bite, but they kicked sand on our faces and we could hear them walking around on the makeshift ceiling.

There weren't enough foxholes to go around so new ones had to be dug. My buddies were digging a hole straight back into the bank when they hit water. Instead of moving, they just put some branches over the water and had running water in their foxhole. There were little tiny fish in that stream, and the guys were always trying to catch them, but I never did see them get any.

We were dug in along a bigger stream in the second position backing up the front line. One night when we were in our foxhole getting ready to go to sleep, we heard the most terrifying scream! As soon as we heard it, everyone sprung into action, grabbing their weapons. Nothing else happened, and I suddenly remembered how earlier that day I had heard a sergeant from down south saying he had a soldier on guard duty that wasn't doing his job like he should. I thought it might have something to do with that.

The next morning the sergeant told us what had happened. The sarge was sure that the soldier didn't have any ammunition in his rifle. The sarge hid along the trail and when the guard came along, he jumped out and grabbed him. That is when we heard the yell. The sarge said the soldier was stronger than he thought he was. He was trying to give him a scare, but the soldier darn near whipped him!

There were thousands of foxholes housing from two to four men each. Normally it was very quiet around there, but we never let our guard down. One morning some of the guys were taking a bath in the stream when shells started raining down. Everyone ran for their foxholes. One fellow was only a few feet from his foxhole when he got a direct hit. We ran right over, but the company aid men were already there, tending to his wounds. One leg was almost completely cut off and he had a hole in his throat, but he could still talk. We took him to the aid station immediately, but sadly, he died shortly after he got there.

There wasn't any place on the beachhead that the Germans couldn't shell or bomb. The danger caused problems for the ships bringing in supplies. They had trouble finding a safe place to keep the supplies. They had them stored in every little ravine or gully that was halfway concealed. From time to time, huge stockpiles of ammunition would be hit. When this happened, we could feel the earth shaking and see flames going up for miles.

CHAPTER 8
The Big Push-Off

The Germans had the high ground and could see the entire beachhead. In order to get ready for the push-off, we had our planes come in and lay a smokescreen to hide what we were doing. Another thing we did was fire off artillery and mortars at different times of the day to throw the Germans off as to what time we were actually going to push off.

We used this time to fortify our lines to get ready for the push-off. They were moving artillery and tanks and whatever other equipment we might need. Also, at night our engineers went out and removed mines that we had placed to stop the Germans. They lay on their stomachs and probed with bayonets. The Germans had put out mines as well, which caused us a lot of trouble. When we were in the middle of a push-off, injured men who had stepped on mines were brought back all day long. We also lost a great number of tanks due to those mines.

There were several kinds of mines. One kind was called anti-personnel, which went off when a person stepped on it. Another kind was bigger and looked like a bowl that was turned over. They covered these with dirt to hide them. When tanks, trucks or any kind of equipment ran over them, they damaged the vehicle so it would no longer operate.

There was one mine called a "Bouncing Betty." When someone stepped on it, it flew up in the air about six feet and then exploded. A person could be killed or seriously wounded. One morning the guys were just sitting down for breakfast near a wooded area. One soldier had just walked over to the serving table and was on his way back with his food when he stepped on a Bouncing Betty. It killed him and wounded 20 others. There were a lot more men killed by artillery than were ever shot. One artillery shell or bomb could kill dozens of men, but a bullet could only kill one.

Mines were always a problem. We never knew when we were going to step on one. Whenever possible, metal detectors were used to find them. Once I saw two officers in a jeep run over a mine. The jeep and the men went up about 15 feet in the air. It killed them both. During the course of the war I walked through several minefields, but never stepped on one. There are places in Europe that are still roped off to prevent people from stepping on mines that were placed there in World War I.

Soon we were getting ready to push off the beachhead and go to Rome. We continued to try to fake out the Germans by shelling in places that we were not really going to be. That way, the Germans didn't know when or where we were going to attack.

The 1st and 3rd battalions pushed off on the 23rd of May. We were lucky that the 2nd Battalion was in reserve. All day long they brought back wounded men who had stepped on mines. They also lost a large number of tanks that ran over mines.

As soon as the 1st and 3rd battalions pushed off, they moved out to fight the Germans and the 2nd Battalion moved up to the position where they had been. It was in a wooded area and by the time we got there, it looked like a hurricane had struck. Large branches and all the leaves had been blown off the trees.

Shell craters were everywhere.

Because of the Germans' heavy artillery, a lot of the men never made it out of the ditch. We saw the bodies of several soldiers who had been killed before they even got to push off. The grave administration crew would collect the dead and take them back to the rear. They had a cemetery on the Anzio Beachhead. After the war the deceased were brought back to the states.

On the evening of the 25th I had just gotten into my foxhole when they said we were moving out. We didn't know where we were going, but we marched most of the night and ended up in a little creek bed in a gully. We were told not to show our heads over the hill. Behind us the hill sloped up quite a ways and we could see a blown up tank.

They told us that at 10am that morning they were going to fire a heavy barrage ahead of us as we pushed off. As we advanced, they would move the artillery ahead of us. There were supposed to be three tanks leading the attack. By 11am the tanks hadn't shown up, so we had to push off without them. Our men had to spread out and go over the hill with no cover whatsoever.

When we got to the top we could see it was just a wheat field. Our first objective was Germans in a canal about 800 yards ahead of us. We were just about 100 feet over the hill when we had our first casualty. The soldier had gotten hit in the jaw. We put him on a stretcher and headed back the way we had come. The problem was that we had no idea where the aid station was. When we got back to where we started from, we saw the three tanks that had been delayed before. One of them was stuck in the creek. The other two were trying to get it out. They weren't much help to us.

The German artillery was trying to hit the tanks. They were coming closer to us. We were laying flat on the ground, but the shells were so close that they were throwing dirt all over us. We wondered how the Germans knew where we were. We found out later there was a German soldier with a radio hiding in a knocked-out tank up on the hill, telling the German artillery where to fire.

We never did find the aid station. We ran across a chemical mortar crew who had a medic with them and said they would take care of our casualty. We agreed and headed back up to the front. By the time we arrived, the infantry had reached its first objective. It was in a deep canal. The canal was quite deep and they had dug rooms into the back.

The Germans had standing foxholes so they could cover the wheat field with machine gun fire. There were casualties all over the battlefield, so we decided that rather than try to move the wounded back one at a time, we would move them to the rooms in the canal. The Germans were still shelling the area. In between barrages, we would go out and pick up wounded men. By nightfall we had over 40 men in there. We hoped to be able to bring up a vehicle to bring them back.

We found out that a vehicle couldn't be brought up, so we started bringing them back one at a time. It was several miles to the aid station. Part of the way was along a canal. After about a mile was a road, and then there was a field that stretched about another mile, until we finally made it to the aid station.

At one point we were on our way back with two wounded men. Just as we were turning off the canal, we met three soldiers from a mortar squad. They were looking for a place to move their mortars closer to the front. After we had dropped off the wounded at the aid station, we ran into these three soldiers again. One of them had been wounded. The other two were carrying him on a makeshift stretcher. They told us that right after they had talked to us one of them had stepped on a mine. We offered to take him back, but they said, "No," that we had more important things to do.

Another time, we had dropped off wounded and were going back to get more, and we came across an MP (military police) on the road. He said we couldn't go through that field because it was full of mines. It was too far to go around, so we figured if we followed the same path we had already been using we would be okay. We were getting very tired by then.

We had been going day and night for several days when a sergeant told us they had brought up a litter squad from the field hospital to give us a rest. We were completely worn out. I had never been so tired in my whole life! We hadn't slept or eaten since the push started.

I sat down to get a bite to eat, and the next thing I knew I was waking up in the middle of the night and someone had thrown a blanket over me. It had fallen off and I was cold. I pulled it back on and went back to sleep. I don't know how long I slept. After we had rested and eaten we went back up to the front line. By that time the Germans were retreating, but the fighting still went on. The division on our right needed some help, so the 2nd Battalion went over to help them.

Charlie Wetzel was part of our litter squad. He was the same age I was, 19. When we had been getting ready to push off the beachhead, they'd needed another medical man, so they had transferred him because he'd had medical training. I heard he'd been transferred to another unit, but later we checked and couldn't find any record of him at all. One morning two of the guys from my litter squad went to look for him and found his body on the beachhead. His body had been burned in the sun. I asked why they didn't wake me up and they said, "It's something you didn't need to see."

We were in a dry creek bed waiting to move out. There was nothing going on, we were just sitting around talking. The creek was about six feet wide and as dry as concrete. The fellow sitting across from me was digging back into the bank to be a little safer in case of shellfire. I would have dug in, too, but I had broken my shovel that morning.

All of a sudden we heard, "BOOM! BOOM!" A German tank had moved to the far end of the creek and was firing point blank at us. The first shell hit halfway between me and the fellow sitting across from me. The whole creek bed was full of smoke. When the smoke cleared, I expected to see wounded men all around me, but no one had been injured! The fellow across from me had his rifle leaned up beside him about a foot away. The barrel of the rifle was bent and all the wood underneath the barrel was blown off, but he didn't have a scratch.

When the second shelling came in we weren't so lucky and several were wounded. We moved the F Company back behind a bombed-out railroad trestle where it was safer, but the E Company, who was closer to the tank, went down into the creek. The tank fired into the high bank above them. It caved in, burying around 30 men.

That was the last fighting we did before we got to Rome.

CHAPTER 9
Rome at Last!

J ust before we arrived in Rome, Italy we came to a large dairy farm. They had just finished milking the cows. I don't think there was a drop of milk remaining by the time we left there. We hadn't had any milk in months.

We arrived at Rome on the 2nd of June. We didn't get to go into Rome on the first day. We came to the Tiber River, where the bridge had been blown up. The combat engineers installed a pontoon bridge so we could get across.

The 3rd Division went right into the center of Rome. We were on the left flank, on the outskirts of the city. We could see St. Peter's Basilica and other impressive buildings, but we had to go on by.

We were stationed in a wheat field about 12 miles outside of Rome. Once we were settled in, we were allowed to go into town quite often. We stayed there about a month. I got to see the Coliseum and go up to the very top of the tower at St. Peter's Basilica. The view was beautiful. It cost me 10 lire, which was about the same as 10 cents.

There were a couple of our guys who seemed to get into trouble whenever they went into town. One day they stole a motorcycle. They had a couple of British officers pushing them to try to get it going, but they could never get it started. One day they got into an argument with a big Canadian sergeant.

The sergeant took one swing at them and knocked them both down. They said it was probably good that they were too drunk to stand back up, or he would have knocked them back down again.

Another time when they went into town they were having a dull day and hadn't gotten into any trouble, so they hitched a ride back with a bunch of soldiers in a jeep. The driver asked if one of them would drive because he wasn't feeling very well. There were guys getting off every so often as they reached their destinations. When they got close to camp they realized that they were the only two left. They parked the jeep at the edge of camp and walked the rest of the way in. The next day the MPs came out to get the jeep. They said it was stolen from a colonel!

On the 6th of June we got word that the troops had landed in Normandy, France. In Anzio, Italy we had done our job occupying as many German troops as possible so they wouldn't be available to fight in Normandy. We thought the war was over. There were rumors that we were going back to the United States to train troops to go to Japan.

Around the 1st of July we got word that we weren't going home. We would be sent down to Salerno, Italy to take amphibious training and to make the invasion into Southern France. Salerno was where the troops had first landed when they'd invaded Italy the year before. We went by truck back to Anzio and got on a ship to take us to Salerno.

CHAPTER 10
Salerno

We were taking our training on the beaches of Salerno where the American troops made their initial invasion of Italy. Our pup tents were set up along the beach just outside the city of Salerno. When I looked out my tent opening, I could see the Isle of Capri. We never got to actually go to the island, but we went by it on our ship.

It was the closest thing to a vacation that I had. Most of the time we didn't have any duties. We could play volleyball or go swimming. Someone had covered part of a stream with canvas so we could bathe privately. Our sergeant had a philosophy that as long as we were available for duty, we could do whatever we wanted while waiting for instructions.

One day the battalion commander came and asked why the men were not training. The sergeant said that we were all on duty. He had a roster with each man's name on it and what we were supposed to be doing. After the commander left our sergeant said, "He can run his battalion the way he wants to, and I'll run my aid station the way I want to."

One of the things I got to do was take a trip to the ancient ruins of Pompeii. Some of the fellows chipped in and we hired a guide to explain about the old ruins. It was very interesting. They had an arena where the Christians fought the lions. There were a lot of outside theaters. The seating areas were like stair steps with places for torches every so often. The streets were made of cobblestones and we could still see the ruts from the chariots.

At the end of the tour we ended up in a big room where they had wine for sale. When you bought wine in Italy, you had to be careful. It might be half kerosene. You could also buy snow cones made with wine.

One morning my buddy and I went to a little restaurant in town. The menu was very simple. Two fried eggs were $1. There was no bread, no water, no coffee, nothing but eggs.

The last of our training was practicing landing on the beach. We would go out and stay overnight on a big ship. The next day we would practice by going down the side of the ship on rope ladders onto small assault boats that were used to land us on the beach.

One day one of the boats landed in an Italian's watermelon patch. He was running around like crazy trying to get everyone out of his watermelon patch. Two medics ended up with a litter piled high with watermelons. They said they had a bunch of wounded.

After we finished our training the entire regiment of approximately 50,000 troops was stationed in a wheat field about 20 miles outside of Naples. We had our aid station set up in an apple orchard, but the apples weren't ripe. It wasn't unusual to wake up in the mornings to the sound of apples hitting the sides of our tents. There was a peach orchard across the road, but they weren't ripe either.

We were divided into areas and each area had a movie screen. If you didn't like the movie being shown you could go over to another area to see what movie they were showing there. They had first-run movies that weren't even shown back in my hometown until after I returned home.

My buddy Bob ran across a couple of infantrymen from F Company that we knew from when we were on the Anzio beachhead. One of the guys asked us, "Do you remember during the push when another litter squad came up to relieve you?"

Apparently just as they got there heavy artillery fire landed in the area. The captain of F Company was hit and seriously wounded. The litter bearers said they couldn't take him back because the artillery was too heavy. One guy said, "I threatened to shoot him if the litter squad didn't take him to the aid station."

The other guy interrupted, saying they probably wouldn't have made it.

The first guy said to us, "A good thing you weren't there, you would have gone."

Then the other guy said, "I don't think you would have made it, but you would have gone. You guys were always there when we needed you." What those infantrymen said to us that night meant more than any medal.

It was starting to get dark so we said goodbye and went back to our own area. As we were walking back, Bob said quietly, "With our luck we might have made it."

We stayed in this location for several weeks waiting for them to get all the material and ships and other supplies ready for us to make the invasion on Southern France. We didn't have much to do, so our sergeant decided that we should go on a hike to build up our muscles. Bob and I didn't think a hike was too good of a deal, so we took off and went to Naples.

When we got there we went to the USO (United Service Organization), and when we went in the front door we heard music coming from upstairs. There was a piano and some other instruments playing. I said to Bob, "That is Leonard Carr playing the piano." Leonard was one of the fellows we took basic training with. He played the piano by ear, and I could tell by the rhythm that it was being played by ear.

We went upstairs, and sure enough, there was Leonard playing the piano. He told us he'd had to make an adjustment in his playing because one of his fingers had been blown off. It had happened when he was in battle and one of the tanks that were supporting the troops fired a shell at the enemy, but as the shell came out of the barrel of the tank, it exploded. A piece of the shell cut Leonard's finger off.

Leonard was a small person, about 5'4" tall. He wore glasses, but that didn't stop him from doing his job. One time he said he had his head turned to the side when a bullet grazed the side of his head and went in and out through his glasses. Though he was wounded several times, he made it through the war and back to the states. He moved back to my hometown and we got together several times after the war.

When we got back from the USO, the other battalions were loading up the supplies and our guys started getting ready to go. While we were waiting at the harbor to get onboard the ship, we saw a big object in the water coming towards the shore. We couldn't tell what it was at first. It ended up being a tank outfitted with what looked like a big life jacket to keep it afloat. It was a sight to see.

Once we were onboard, we had to wait several days for all of the supplies and men to be loaded on to the ships. There were three divisions involved in the landing, which meant there were thousands of men and hundreds of ships. The Navy was also involved. Battleships offshore were not only transporting the Army, but also giving them support.

In the midst of waiting, we heard that two men were missing from roll call. They had not boarded the ship with everyone else. One day we saw a rowboat coming from the shore. It was the two missing men. They had hired an Italian man to row them out to the ship. We never found out what they had been doing, but I bet it was more fun that what we had been doing.

The ship we were on was loaded with supplies and barrels of gasoline. There were no accommodations for troops. We slept wherever we could find a spot. One of the things I was assigned to take ashore was a stretcher with two blankets on it, so I was much better off than most because I had my own bed with me. I set my bed up on top of a barrel of gasoline because there was nowhere else to put it.

The trip took about two days. As we went by the island of Corsica one of the guys had an appendicitis attack, so they put him ashore on a small boat. On the 15th of August when I woke up, we were sitting off the shore of Southern France, ready to make our landing.

CHAPTER 11
Southern France

When we were on the ship preparing to go to France they showed us aerial photographs of where we were going to land. There was a highway running along parallel to the ocean. The aerial photos showed a seawall between the ocean and the highway. Every so many men were given a ladder about 10 feet high to use to get over the seawall. The seawall was different heights. Where we landed the seawall was about four feet high. Some of the guys were wondering what the heck we were doing with those ladders.

While we were sitting offshore we could observe our planes dropping bombs. The smaller boats had rows of rockets. We watched them run in parallel to the shore and fire them - "Boom, boom, BOOM!"

There were also several battleships supporting the invasion. The battleship Texas would fire its big guns at the beach. It was sitting out a little farther than we were. The concussions just about knocked us over.

While we were waiting to go in they fed us a hot breakfast.

The groups were going in on what we called waves, and the waves were about two minutes apart. We went in on the sixth wave. We climbed down rope ladders into assault boats, and then circled around until it was our time to go in. All the boats in our wave spread out to make a line going onto the beach.

They told us to keep our heads down but we couldn't resist peeking up to take a look.

The medics were spread out among the groups. We were told to take enough supplies for three days. I carried my supplies in my large canvas vest. Having been in combat before, we knew that we didn't want to bring along anything at all that we didn't need. Some of the guys that didn't know any better were bringing packs full of everything they could think of.

We were a little surprised because when our boat pulled onto the shore, nobody was even shooting at us. We were able to pull up right onto the beach. We didn't even get our feet wet. Our landing wasn't any different than the practice ones in Italy except that this time we didn't run into a watermelon patch.

The beach ended just past the highway, and then we had to go up a hill following after the first group. We didn't have any trouble figuring out where they had gone because the whole hillside was littered with those heavy packs that they had thrown off because of the extra weight.

We hadn't gone too far when one of the riflemen got his gun caught on a branch and shot himself in the leg. We had to take him back down to the beach, and when we got there another wave was coming in. We saw our fellow medics and joined up with them, so that made seven medics together including our captain, who was the only doctor we had for the whole detachment.

This put us quite a ways behind the rest of our original wave. When they went into combat they would string a telephone wire behind them. We figured if we followed the telephone wire we could catch up to them. On the way we found a couple of other soldiers that were separated from their units. One of the men had a carbine rifle and one had a .45 pistol. Since medics weren't allowed to carry guns, these were the only guns we had with us.

By this time it was getting dark. We came across a little stone shed and decided to spend the night there. We were up on the hill above where we had landed, and that night the German planes came in and started bombing the convoy of ships. It looked like a 4th of July celebration! The anti-aircraft shells and what they call tracer bullets were streaming across the night sky. They are called tracers because you can see the trail they make. That was the end of our first day in France.

There was a lot of noise, but we heard the next day that there wasn't much damage. We got up early in the morning with the intent of catching up with the rest of the troops. There was no one around, so we continued following the telephone wire down the path. After a couple of hours we came to the end of the wire. We assumed that they had continued down the path that we had been following. The captain said, "Let's take a break before we go on." Two of the guys said they didn't need to rest and would go on ahead.

After we took a break we continued along the side of the mountain. Where the path straightened out there was a big rock. The rock was so big we couldn't see around it. Just as we reached the rock we heard an explosion. It sounded like mortar fire, so the captain said we would take another break. It had been about an hour of rough terrain since our last break.

About that time, one of the two guys who had gone ahead came back around the rock with his gun shaking in his hand. He said there were a bunch of Germans coming down the trail.

We had no place to go. If we went back the way we came, we would be exposed. I can still remember the captain's voice saying, "Just give them your name, rank and serial number."

The Germans didn't come around the rock. They were close enough that we could hear them talking, but instead of coming around the rock they went up the other side of the canyon. We counted 14 of them. They had a machine gun and they all had weapons.

There were seven of us and five were medics. The two that were not medics had been separated from the rest of their party, and they were the only ones who had guns. The guy with the rifle stood up and was going to shoot at the Germans. Fortunately his gun didn't fire; it just went, "click." He didn't get a chance to shoot again. We grabbed him and pulled him down and told him if he wanted to fight a German patrol, not to do it when we were around.

After we stayed there for about an hour, the captain said that we should get moving. We went around the rock and down the trail about a quarter of a mile. We came across two soldiers who had built a small fire and were drinking coffee. We asked them if they had seen any Germans. They said there had been some a little while ago but they had run them off.

We were lost. We had no idea where we were, so we continued on down the path, finally coming to a road. We heard a vehicle coming. The captain said to stay down until we knew if it was one of ours, or if it was the enemy. It turned out to be two Americans in a jeep. They told us that if we walked about another mile we would come to the beach. There we could get a ride with a truck back up to the front.

When we got up to the front there was quite a battle going on. Some of our medics that had arrived with another group had set up an aid station in an old winery. Just after we got there a soldier was wounded standing in the doorway of the aid station.

On down the road about half a mile one of our tanks had been hit by an anti-tank gun and was burning. The tank driver said that he and the assistant driver had crawled out into a ditch. The Germans were shooting at them with machine guns. He said had he crawled in the ditch all the way back, but he didn't know what had happened to the assistant driver. It's a small world out there. The tank driver and one of the medics were next door neighbors back in their hometown and neither one had known the other was in the service.

The Germans had installed a 20ml anti-aircraft gun in the hills above our station and were firing it at us like a machine gun. When a 20ml shell hits, it explodes! I got behind a big wall with another guy, thinking we would be safe there, but we didn't take into account the explosions. We were standing under a tree when one of the shells hit the top of the tree and exploded. When it hit, the tree split and shrapnel went flying everywhere. The other guy suffered a bad injury in his shoulder, but I didn't have a scratch on me. That ended our second day in France.

CHAPTER 12
More of My Experiences in France

These are further experiences I had while in France, but I can't guarantee this is the exact order they happened in.

On the 6th day in France we came to a river. You could see all along the banks where our planes had dropped bombs trying to blow up the bridge. When we came to the bridge we could see that one bomb had hit right in the middle of it, leaving a big hole, but the bridge was still standing. We could cross on foot, but we couldn't bring any heavy equipment across. When we crossed over, we ran into some French allies. They told us there were German tanks were headed right for us. Thank goodness, they never showed up. The combat engineers quickly built a pontoon bridge. The materials to repair the bridge weren't due for 21 days.

The next thing I remember was the first French town we fought in. We had our aid station in a barn about two miles from the town. It was nice to have dry straw for a bed. When I woke up there were chickens on my chest. Over in the corner they had a pen with two mules. They were the biggest mules I had ever seen. They reminded me of the draft horses that pull beer wagons. One soldier came into the barn in the middle of the night and didn't know he was in the pen with the mules. When he woke up in the morning, the mules were huddled up in the corner to keep from stepping on him.

At about 10am that same morning, we learned that there were two wounded men in the town. My litter squad was sent to bring them back to the aid station. We had a rifleman show us the way. When we got to the town there was a bridge going over a little creek. Instead of going over the bridge we went through the creek bed so the Germans wouldn't see us. When we arrived opposite the house where F Company was fighting, there was quite a large open space between the creek and the house. We ran as fast as we could and didn't get shot at.

When we came into the house the first person we saw was the sergeant. He asked, "What are you doing here?"

We replied, "We came to pick up the wounded." He said the building we were in was surrounded, and there were Germans in the house next door.

This was a typical French house in a small town. Most of the farmers lived in town and farmed the land around town. The house and the barn were one building. On one side was a barn with a hayloft and on the other side was a house with a second story. The wounded men were in the barn. Bob and I went up into the hayloft as lookouts to see what was going on. We could see E Company trying to get into the middle of town.

We were up in this hayloft and could hear the artillery shells going over us. We heard one shell coming and we knew it wasn't going to make it to the far end of town. It hit the roof of the house we were in. We were lucky we were in the hayloft and not the house.

Shortly we heard someone yelling, "Medic!"

Bob and I went downstairs in the barn and then back upstairs in the house. There were two wounded men in the attic. You could see where the shell had hit the tile roof and shattered it into hundreds of pieces. The wounds weren't very serious, but there were so many that it took nearly all the bandages we had. We took them back down into the barn where the rest of the men were.

Just as we got back into the barn, a rifleman came in and told us the Germans were coming around and starting to close in on us. One soldier said we could drop hand grenades out the windows of the hayloft. That was a good idea, but no one had any hand grenades.

The Germans began firing machine gun bullets through the barn door. We laid down flat on the ground and no one got hit. I got behind a big sack of feed, and then I remembered that I had some German money. I didn't want to be caught with it, so I hid it in the sack of feed. Things were looking pretty bad. None of our riflemen had more than about eight bullets left.

Amazingly, at that time one of our tanks came up behind the house firing away. The sarge hollered at the tank driver which way to fire, but the driver said he had run out of ammunition. Even so, I think he saved the day, because the Germans pulled back when they saw the tank.

Because we were out of ammunition, we got permission to pull out. We had a problem, though. We had three wounded, but only two stretchers. It was quite a distance of open space from the house to the creek, so we decided to take two of the wounded across the open space down into the creek bed, and then we went back for the other wounded soldier.

The infantrymen covered us while we went back and forth before they came themselves. We were lucky no one got hurt.

After everyone pulled out, we covered the town with artillery fire. Once all the Germans were gone, we went back into town. The streets were lined with French people, who were hollering and cheering. I don't know where they had been during all the firing.

We got word that there was a wounded soldier laying in the field so we hopped into a jeep and went to pick him up. It was one of our medics, a young kid from Chicago. His leg was shattered and he could hardly move, but every time a shell hit nearby, it made him jump, causing intense pain. I noticed he had his helmet lying nearby. When he picked it up, I saw that he had a picture of his wife and child inside. We took him back to the aid station like nothing out of the ordinary had just happened.

CHAPTER 13
Grenoble

We weren't too far from Grenoble, France. Our medical officer had studied medicine in Grenoble for seven years. He knew everyone in the town and was disappointed we were not planning to go there. We got word that morning, however, that as soon as we secured the town we were in, we would in fact be going to Grenoble.

While we were waiting to go to Grenoble, some of us were hanging out in the courtyard behind the aid station, which was a little house with a back porch. I was sitting wrapped up in a blanket and reading a book, about 20 feet away from the door. I wasn't at the end of a page or a chapter. I don't know why, but I decided to stop reading and go inside.

When I got to the door, the captain was coming out. I opened the door for him, and he stepped outside just as I was about to step in. He was at the end of the porch when three shells hit in the area. One hit where the captain was, one hit where I had been reading the book and another one hit close to that same area. I fell inside the building. The captain was lying on the porch. The guys hurried him into the aid station, but he had been killed almost immediately.

The captain was our doctor, and our detachment only had one medical officer. When he was killed, it shook everyone up. It took several days to get another doctor, and the dentist filled in during that time.

I was pretty shaken up, thinking, "Why him?" He was the only person in the whole division who cared that we go to Grenoble and he had just missed it.

Then I heard a voice inside my head, as clear as day, saying, "I say who and I say when." I was reminded that God made the decisions and I never questioned Him after that. I went back out into the yard where I had been reading the book, and the blanket was ripped to shreds. That is one thing I will never forget.

Two days later we were in Grenoble, and I was thinking about how the captain never made it. We didn't have to do any fighting while we were there.

When we left Grenoble, the whole 20-mile long convoy crossed the French Alps driving blackout, with no lights at all. It was so dark you couldn't see anything, but we could feel when we went around the curves.

The medical core had two vehicles, a jeep pulling a trailer, and a ¾-ton truck. The truck was loaded with supplies and equipment covered with a tarp. Some of us were riding on top of the tarp holding onto each other to keep from falling off. The next day we came back over the same road in the daytime. If I had known the night before how narrow the road was with its steep drop off, I would have gotten out and walked.

After that, we were moving through towns so fast it was hard to keep track of where we were. The next town I remember was Rambervillers in northeastern France. We were there for a few days. The infantrymen were dug in about 1½ miles from town. We had our aid station set up in the factory area of town, so if we needed to, we could get to where they were if anyone was wounded.

Someone had a baseball and a mitt. I was playing catch when the ball hit my hand, which made me drop it. I stepped on it, hurting my ankle, and I had to be helped into the aid station. It hurt quite a bit and my ankle was starting to swell. One of the aid station staff told me I didn't need to go to the hospital, and that they would take care of me there. He wrapped an elastic bandage around my ankle.

I was in a lot of pain when I noticed a French girl of about 10 years old, who was holding my hand with tears streaming down her face. I needed that. No one likes to cry alone, and I had a few tears too. I don't know where she came from or where she went. I'll never forget the day I fell in love with a little French girl who was there when I needed her.

The next day we were called up to the front. Even though my ankle was swollen and hurt like the dickens, four of us went and picked up a boy about my age, 19. He had gotten hit in the rear end. We joked with him about how he would get to go home because he had gotten hit in the butt. Later that day I asked how he was doing and was told that he had died. They told me that a piece of shrapnel had gone up into a vital organ. We felt bad about kidding him, but maybe it wasn't so bad that we had. It probably took his mind off things a little bit.

A couple of days later the infantry decided to push on, so we moved the aid station closer to the front. We set up inside a little house. When we first went in, we saw a backpack with the emblem of a major. Sticking out of the bag was a cribbage board. The major probably wondered what happened to his cribbage board, but we figured he could get a new one easier than we could. We only took the cribbage board. We never even opened the pack.

We came to a little town where all the civilians had gone, but there were quite a few rabbits and chickens running around. Three of us decided to fry up some chickens in one of the houses. Anyone that came along, we would give a piece of chicken to.

When we were exploring the upstairs of the house, we saw a large unexploded artillery shell lying by a potbelly stove. It looked like it might have come in through the window, but we knew it hadn't because if it had, it would have made a dent in the floor. We went downstairs and cooked some more chicken.

CHAPTER 14

80+ Days on the Line

From the 15th of August to the 10th of November 1944, we were on the front line in southern France. Around the 1st of November, we started hearing rumors that a new division was coming to relieve us, and after a break, we would be going to the German border.

When we were relieved, we told the new guys that it had been raining and cold and everything was muddy. One of our soldiers told his replacement, "You can have my foxhole. It has all the comforts of home, if you like a leaky roof and about two feet of water."

They took our whole battalion in 10 trucks back to the rear. We were off of the front line from the 10th of November to the day before Thanksgiving. It was nice to have some time off to just relax and do nothing. We got to stay in a little school with beds. I remember that there was a celebration for Armistice Day. They even had a band! We got a Thanksgiving dinner with turkey and all the trimmings the day before Thanksgiving. The next day we were headed back to the front.

There were about 90 men in each rifle company when we first started out. The 2nd Battalion consisted of E, F and G companies. When we were relieved, there were only about 26 men left in E Company. That had been our largest company. They replenished our troops before we left again.

When we went back up to the front they took us in trucks again. We could tell when we were getting close to the front because we started driving by smoking vehicles and dead bodies. The area between France and Germany was called Alsace-Lorraine. Some of the road signs were written in German and some in French.

We crossed into Germany for the first time on the 15th of December. Someone had put up a sign that said, "Welcome to Germany! Spit on Hitler's Home!" But they had misspelled spit "S-H-I-T". Haha!

They sent the battalion up to take a town named Bundenthal. The town was in a valley in western Germany. The Germans had the high ground around the town. Some of our soldiers headed for a barn, the others headed for houses and other buildings.

I headed for the barn, and a soldier who was already there told me the following story. The Germans were shooting downhill at the barn and they were shooting uphill at the Germans. The Germans started firing tracer bullets. They are very hot and started some of the hay on fire. The men had to stop shooting to put the fires out and then start shooting again.

After we had been in Bundenthal for a while, the Germans stopped firing, but still had the town surrounded. We had little hope that some of the Americans would ever get back to their own lines again. On the 23rd of December, two men made it back to where we were. They said there were 70 men stranded in the town. They were low on medical supplies, food and ammunition. They were eating potato peelings and rotten apples. They had found a goose, but they were saving it for Christmas dinner if they didn't get rescued. It might have been their last meal.

Rescue plans were made to go get them as soon as possible. The plan was to go in at about 1am on the 24th. Just before we went in, our artillery fired rounds at the high ground where they thought the Germans might be. The patrol made it to where the trapped and injured men were, and evacuated them with no resistance. All 70 men were brought back safely.

The next day we heard that the litter bearers from the 1st and 3rd battalions got Silver Stars for volunteering to go on this dangerous mission. We asked, "Why didn't we get Silver Stars?"

They responded, "Because you didn't volunteer." As opposed to the other battalions, we had been commanded.

The next day was Christmas. Things quieted down. We were staying in a small town. On Christmas Eve I got two packages. One was a book from my aunt. The other was something to eat, but I don't remember what it was. Santa can find you no matter where you are.

For Christmas dinner we had turkey with dressing and all the trimmings. It's not quite the same as home when you are eating out of a mess kit. We never found out what happened to the goose.

The day after Christmas we got word that there were two wounded men on the line. They were in a foxhole at the top of a hill. It was quite a job getting up the hill. The two men in the foxhole had accidentally shot both of themselves in the foot with one bullet. We told them we didn't care if they had shot themselves, but we hoped they would walk down that big hill. Of course we ended up carrying them.

CHAPTER 15
The Start of a New Year - 1945

We were in a little town just inside the German border. We had an ambulance attached to our unit, which they rotated every few days. We didn't have any wounded to send back.

Somebody jokingly asked, "Is there anybody sick?"

I felt great, but I told them I was sicker than a dog, so they put a tag on me and put me in the ambulance. I figured I would just have a ride to the hospital and come right back on the next ambulance.

Much to my surprise, when I got off the ambulance I saw a doctor that I knew. He asked me what I was doing there. I told him and he said, "You might as well stay around a few days and rest up." He said if anybody came around asking questions, he would take care of it.

The hospital was in a Catholic church back in France. There were nuns there. One of them asked me if I needed some help taking my "shoosies" off. I lay around for a couple of days eating good food.

Then we got word that there was a battle happening on a bulge. It became the famous "Battle of the Bulge." We were told to pull back, level out our line and dig in. They had to move the hospital back, so everybody that could walk was sent back to the front.

When I got back, they asked, "Where have you been?"

I said, "I was sick."

We had a problem. The Germans had attacked us with troops they had brought down from the Russian front. We were told not to use any more ammunition than we needed to because they were sending everything they could up to the bulge.

The only ones in the town were the forward command post and our medic station. They wanted a litter squad there. We were staying in a big stone house right across the street from where the battalion headquarters were. Right behind the house was a little courtyard where they had chemical mortars set up so they could support the troops on the line.

We stayed in the basement, which is usually the safest place to be. There were some potatoes stored in there, so we decided to have french fries. We had a little potbelly stove that we carried with us in the jeep. We set it up down in the basement with the pipe smoke going out the window. We usually had an extra canteen of grease.

They had run a phone line into our building so they could contact us if they needed to. Everyone was on the same line from the headquarters across the street to the guys on the front line. We all had a different ring - it might be five rings or nine. When the phone started ringing, I always held my breath to see if it was our ring or if it was going to go on past. We took turns being on phone duty.

One night when I was on duty, all of a sudden someone was shaking me; I guess I had dozed off. He said he had been trying to get us on the phone. He had followed the phone line all the way from the battalion. When he got to me, I was asleep and the line was pulled out from the phone. He wasn't very happy.

Since everybody was on the same phone line, we could all hear everything that was going on. One night I heard soldiers from the front asking for more mortar support. The mortar crew said they didn't like to fire at night and give away their position.

The reply was, "We need support NOW!"

The mortar was set up in the courtyard right behind where we were staying. I could hear the mortars firing behind us and I could hear the shells hitting on the front through the phone.

I went across to headquarters to see what was going on. Half the town was on fire. Just as I stepped into a building across the street, something that had been burning in the middle of the street about a block down blew up.

The next thing I heard was, "Move a little to the right and keep firing. You're doing good." It was one of our soldiers who had asked for support letting the mortar crew know they were hitting the targets.

It didn't take us long to realize our house was on fire, so we went back to town, where the main aid station was. When we came back the next morning, our house was completely collapsed and just a pile of rubbish.

They were still fighting just outside the edge of town, so we went back to the main aid station instead of operating from the forward position. One night we got a call that someone was wounded in F Company, so Bill McDermott and I went to pick up the wounded man.

The troops were dug in on the backside of a fairly steep hill. Bill was ahead of me. About the time we were almost to the top, German artillery shells started hitting the hill. One of the soldiers in a foxhole hollered at me to get into the foxhole with him, so I jumped in.

The shelling didn't last long. When it stopped, I crawled out and started back up the hill. I heard someone come up behind me. It was Bill. I said, "I thought you were right behind me."

He said, "I had just gotten to the top of the hill when a shell hit so close to me it knocked me right off!"

I asked him if he was all right. He said his back was a little sore, but he was okay to go on. We put the wounded man on the stretcher and took him back to the aid station.

It was 4am when we got back to the aid station and we were tired out! We had just sat down when the sergeant came in and said there was another wounded man. We started to get up to go back up the hill when the sergeant told us he would send other men. We were so glad, because we were exhausted. We would have gone, though. No matter how tired we were, we always went where we were needed.

One night we got word there was a wounded man up on the hill, so I took my litter squad and went up to get him. He was down in the bottom of a foxhole and we knew it was going to be trouble getting him out. Some of the guys were arguing about how to get him out. I told them no matter how we did it, it was going to hurt him, and we better hurry or it would be us that needed to be pulled out.

I got down into the hole and moved him around until the others could get a hold of his shoulders, and I supported his back while they pulled him out. We did it pretty quickly, so I don't think it hurt him too much. We carried him back down the hill to the aid station in the dark.

Around the beginning of February a new division that had just come over from the states relieved us. Our division was getting pulled off the line to get ready for the big push-off scheduled for the 15th of March.

Just as we were ready to move out, we got word that the new division was having trouble securing the hill outside of town. Every time they would attack, the Germans would counterattack and push them off the hill. We got orders to be ready in 30 minutes to go give them support. In less than an hour after we had gotten our orders, we had secured the hill. I think it helped that we were a seasoned outfit, while they were fresh from the states.

Instead of moving out right away, we decided to stick around in case the new division needed help. The whole battalion moved into different French houses. My litter squad and I stayed with a nice, elderly French couple. They had a spare room where the four of us slept in sleeping bags at night. The old French man had been in WWI. He got out his uniform and showed it to us. He was quite proud of it.

The house was heated by an old potbelly stove in the living room. We would go out and get wood for it. They had a big kitchen, but we had to go to the battalion kitchen to get our food. We always brought back enough to feed the couple, too.

The old woman said she had a lot of apples and she'd make us a pie, but she didn't have any sugar. We told her, "No problem! Get us a list of what you need and we'll get it."

She made us a French apple pie. It was the first and only time I ever had a homemade French apple pie made by a French woman out of French apples. We also heard that another French man had a calf for sale. We pooled our money with the kitchen crew and bought it. We shared it with the kitchen crew and the French people.

One day we were eating in the kitchen when we heard a loud explosion in the dining room. We rushed in to see what had happened. Someone had left an unopened can of beans on top of the stove. There were beans on the wall, beans on the ceiling, beans on the floor, beans pretty much everywhere! We all chipped in and helped clean up the mess. Nobody ever 'fessed up to leaving it there, though. Apparently no one knew how it got there.

When we got ready to leave everyone was sad. I think the old woman had a few tears in her eyes.

CHAPTER 16
The Push-Off to Germany

Living On Borrowed Time

After we left the old couple's home, they pulled us off the line to get our replacements in and get us ready for the big push-off to Germany. We headed out on the 15th of March 1945.

The place we stayed looked like a hotel, and a train track ran near it. It was likely a place for people to stay when they had to layover waiting for the next train. It was nice to have a soft bed to sleep in. A fireplace heated each room, so we went out and cut wood to keep warm.

There was a man-made lake nearby that looked like a gravel pit. We decided to see if we could get a couple of fish. Someone had a few hand grenades, so we rowed out in a boat, pulled the pins, and threw the hand grenades down into the water. They didn't make a lot of noise, just a kind of "poof!" This didn't result in any fish, so we needed to come up with a Plan B.

Someone had the idea to use a landmine. They were shaped just like 2x4s. The way they were normally used was to place one in the middle of a road and cover it up so it could not be seen. There was a detonator with a wire running over it to set it off when someone drove across it.

In this case, we fastened the detonator to the landmine and lowered it into the water, rowed back to shore, and set it off with a battery we had. Unlike the grenades, this explosion made a lot of noise and the water came rushing onto the shore like a tidal wave. We were a little disappointed when we rowed back out to get all the fish. We only found three or four small, dead fish. We decided the lake must have been fished out before we got there.

We were scheduled to push through the 71st Infantry, which was holding the line at the front. We were expecting a lot of casualties, so they brought another litter squad up from the field hospital to help us. As soon as the infantry moved out, we litter squads moved right into the position where they had been on the edge of the woods.

In front of the woods for maybe half a mile was open country. There was a small hill beyond this and we could hear rifle fire going off in that direction. We waited a while, and then a rifleman came back and said they had two wounded. I turned to the leader of the squad from the field hospital and told him it was time to go. He said, "No!"

He thought we should stay where we were. I told him it was different than in the field hospital where the wounded were brought to you. Out here we had to go get them. I asked the other three men in my squad if they were ready to go, and they also said no. They thought we should stay there, too.

I took two stretchers and gave one to the rifleman and told him that maybe we could get someone to help us bring the wounded back. It was quite a long walk to get up the hill to where they were fighting, but there was no one shooting at us, no shells falling around us, and it was a surprisingly peaceful walk.

When we got up to the hill they were fighting behind, the rifleman said, "You stay here and I'll go see what the situation is."

While I was waiting I heard a noise. It was the other three men from my litter squad who had decided to come up. I asked about the litter squad from the field hospital, and they said they had gone back. Just then the rifleman showed up and said, "You guys get out of here, the Germans are counterattacking!"

We started the long walk back to the wooded area. One of the men in the litter squad said, "If you guys aren't going to run, get out of the way so I can!"

We waited at the edge of the woods again. After quite awhile, the rifleman came and said the German attack had been repelled, and it was now safe to come get the wounded. We trudged back to where the fighting had been and retrieved the two wounded soldiers. We took them back to the aid station, but didn't see hide or hair of the other litter squad.

The next day we came to The Siegfried Line. It was the German's main line of defense to protect their homeland.

CHAPTER 17
The Siegfried Line

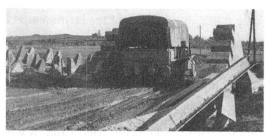

The German's main line of defense for defending their homeland had been built many years before. They had cleared a big area of land in northern France. The Siegfried Line was almost 400 miles long. We had hundreds of soldiers trying to make it across this line.

Along the cleared space on the line they had what were called dragon's teeth. They looked like pyramid-shaped gravestones, pointed so they resembled teeth. They were about three feet high. Their purpose was to stop tanks, self-propelled guns, trucks and any other kind of vehicle. They had trenches dug just beyond the dragon's teeth. They called them anti-tank ditches. If someone were to get through the dragon's teeth, they would get stuck in the trenches. Several hundred feet beyond this were the pillboxes.

The Germans had built what were called pillboxes out of cement, with domes on top. Each one was big enough to bring an anti-tank weapon into through the steel door on the backside. There were holes cut out of the front to put guns through to shoot, but the cement protected the guns and men inside. They built them in groups of three so they could have each other's backs. There were trenches between them so they could go back and forth. There were hundreds of them.

Our engineers blasted the dragon's teeth, and then filled the trenches with dirt. That way they could bring their armory up to support the troops trying to take the pillboxes on foot. The division headquarters estimated it would take as long as six months to get through the line. The actual time it took to break through was less than a week.

We had to cross a large open space to get to the wounded. When we got to one of the pillboxes that our guys had taken over, a soldier was crying out, "Hurry up! Hurry up!"

We asked why and he said, "Didn't you notice the bullets flying all around you?"

We had been running as fast as we could already, and didn't stop to see if we were being shot at.

We evacuated a lot of wounded. I don't remember how many, but I do remember going to pick up a wounded soldier later on in the week when the troops had moved further into the German line. We didn't have any trouble crossing the line to the first row of pillboxes because that row had already been taken. The Germans had connected all the pillboxes with trenches about four feet deep and just wide enough to walk in.

Since the shelling had started up again, we decided to walk down in the trenches. At one point I looked up over the edge and saw a shell hit the ground and skip along like a stone skipping over water. Since the shell didn't explode, it was likely an armor-piercing shell fired from a tank. They would only explode if they hit something hard, like a tank or the side of a pillbox.

We continued on up the trench until we came to the front line, but when we arrived, the wounded man had already been taken back. The other litter bearers decided to stay and talk to a couple of their buddies who they found there. I told them I was going to go on back.

The shelling had stopped for the moment, so I decided to walk along the top of the trench. If the shelling started again I could always hop down into the trench where it was safer. As I was walking along, I looked over and saw one German standing alone beside a pillbox. I decided to go over and see what was up with him. When I got over to the pillbox I told him to come with me.

He said, "Nein."

I told him again to come. He pointed to the pillbox and said, "Comrades."

I told him to get his comrades and come. I heard them arguing. I looked back over at the trench and 12 Germans came out with their hands up. It was too far to make a run for it. I lined them up and searched them to see if they had any weapons. The only weapon I had was a stretcher.

About that time the rest of my litter squad came along. A rifleman had come with them in case the pillboxes still had any Germans in them. That is how I got credit for capturing 12 Germans on my own. It was a brave thing for me to do, but there is a fine line between bravery and stupidity.

A few days later we went back to pick up another wounded man. We could drive a jeep right up to where he was. Just as we got there, we got word that the Germans had pulled off of the Siegfried Line. We saw a couple of bicycles by the side of the road, so we told the jeep driver to go ahead and take him back and we would ride the bicycles into town.

It was a pleasant ride, mostly downhill. We were enjoying the sunshine and the fact that nobody was shooting at us. We didn't see any soldiers. We figured that the troops must be at the other end of town, so we turned and went up a side street. We didn't see anybody, so we decided to go back the way we had come. On the way back we met some infantrymen coming toward us. They asked us if we had seen any German troops.

We said, "No."

They said they had been told to clear all the Germans out of that end of town. We told them we had already done it.

CHAPTER 18
Springtime

The next place we ran into the enemy, they were dug into the high ground along a road. Our troops knew it was going to be pretty hard to get past them to the next town. We had to go down a road that was under observation by the Germans. It was decided we would dig in for a couple of days to get organized and plan how to proceed.

Our aid station was in a town alongside a river. It was springtime and the river was flooding. There were two bridges across the river. The road crossing the big bridge that the vehicles could go over couldn't be used during the daytime because it was in the German's line of sight.

The litter bearers had to cross a small bridge, which had about eight inches of water that had flooded across the top of it. We went through water up to our ankles. After crossing the bridge, the two of us could go on up to the woods without the Germans seeing us. It took about three hours roundtrip from the front to the aid station.

Our feet didn't get wet, though, because we had pack shoes. The bottoms were made like rubber overshoes with leather above that. They kept your feet dry, but they were uncomfortable to walk in. They had a felt inner sole to absorb sweat because the shoes were so tight your feet would get hot. I had a spare set of inner soles so I could change them out when my feet got sweaty. I carried the spare set in my shirt so they could dry out during the day.

One evening just as it was getting dark we were called on to go back to the front to pick up a wounded man. Another road had been cleared out so we could drive up to the front without being observed by the Germans. There were the two of us litter bearers and a jeep driver. The battalion had set up a forward command post on the way there. We stopped and asked them the location of the wounded man. They told us we could drive up only so far, and then we would have to park the jeep and walk the rest of the way, so that's what we did.

We were quite surprised when we got there to find another jeep. The driver of that jeep said that if one of us would go with him to take care of the wounded man, then we wouldn't have to carry him all the way back to our jeep. I said I would go, as I was the leader of our litter squad. The jeep driver then changed his mind and said he thought he could handle the wounded man alone, and I could just walk back with the other litter bearer and our jeep driver. They had already headed back, and by the time I got to where our jeep had been parked I could see them driving off.

I had a decision to make. I could either walk back up to the front and hope I would get there in time to go back with that jeep driver, or I could walk back to the command post and catch a ride from there. Fearing that I would not get back up to the front in time to get a ride with that jeep, I decided to walk back to the command post. It was a longer walk back to the command post, but if I missed the jeep at the front, I would have to walk back to the command post all the way from there.

As I was walking down the path in the woods, I heard someone walking down the trail toward me. Thinking it was our men, but not knowing for sure, I crouched down in the bushes. It was our men, but I remained hidden and they never knew I was there.

When I got back to the command post there was a soldier walking back and forth on guard duty. I swung around behind him and he never saw me until I was right upon him. I told him he was lucky I wasn't a German or he would have been dead.

At the command post they didn't have any jeeps going into town that night. There was a pile of sleeping bags nearby waiting to be taken to the front, so I decided to get into one and spend the night. Just as I got into the sleeping bag, I heard a jeep. They were going into town, so I hitched a ride with them to the aid station.

The infantry was going to push off the next day before day-light. They wanted to go while it was still dark because they had to go down a road where they might be observed. They gathered in one area so they could eat breakfast and collect what supplies and ammunition they needed for the next battle. While they were getting ready, in came a load of artillery shells. The men being so concentrated, about 20 of them were wounded.

It was still dark, so we could use the main road to bring our ambulance up and get the wounded. We put as many into the ambulance as we could. We told the driver to take those men directly back to the hospital, not to the aid station. It was more than we could handle there.

After the ambulance left, we could take two at a time back to the aid station in the jeep. It was starting to get light out, so we figured we could make maybe three trips back before it was completely light out, and after it got light we would only be able to carry them back one at a time on foot. We had more than three trips to make, but then a fog set in and we couldn't see 10 feet ahead of us. We figured if we hurried we could make a couple more trips with the jeep before the fog lifted. Just as we got back to the aid station with the last two men, the fog lifted and it was a beautiful, sunny day. I was thinking about how God had parted the Red Sea, and if He could do that, He could make a fog to protect us.

Due to all the problems, it was decided we wouldn't push off until the next morning. We hoped to push off before daylight and make it to the next town while it was still dark. We got word that they had a wounded soldier in the town. We went in a jeep with the two of us litter bearers and the jeep driver. We thought if we were fast we could make it over there and back before the sun came up.

We were driving down the road about as fast as the jeep could go. We hit a shell crater in the road and we were airborne! We landed out in a field about 20 feet from the road. The jeep didn't turn over; it landed on all four wheels and bounced around like a rubber ball. The three of us large men were packed into the front of the jeep pretty tight, so none of us fell out. We had a rack on the back to carry two stretchers. The rack was broken. We had a piece of rope to tie the rack back together. We got back on the road, made it to the town and picked up the wounded before daylight.

CHAPTER 19
Aschaffenburg

After leaving the Siegfried line, the 2nd and 3rd battalions headed for the Rhine River. We crossed the Rhine at Frankfurt, Germany. We heard that General Patton's Third Army had already been there and secured the area.

At the edge of Frankfurt along the river, we came to a warehouse full of liquor that the Germans had brought to Paris. Pretty soon no one had water in their canteens, and food rations were thrown out to make way for more liquor in the trucks. For a while every hour was happy hour.

We got word that Patton had captured Aschaffenburg and wanted the 45th Division to come and occupy it. Patton had captured a railroad bridge across the river, the only bridge that hadn't been blown up. They left an anti-aircraft gun there to protect it from German planes.

It was a nice day and we were driving along, when all of a sudden there were bullets whizzing around us, so we jumped out of the jeep into a ditch. As we were hunkered down there, we heard a "sss" noise and noticed that the air was going out of one of the tires on the jeep. It had run over shrapnel. Dodging bullets, we ran up to the top of a hill.

Then the troops noticed that there were no white surrender flags flying through the windows of the town. Because of this, the attacking troops were on high alert. It's well that they were;

later we found out that a German major had organized the town to fight until the last person was dead or captured. All the white flags were ordered down or there would be punishment. They intended to hold up the American troops as long as possible.

The townspeople had been given an opportunity to leave. They had a certain amount of time to comply or they would be caught in the crossfire. We had to fight room to room. We had to fight for every foot we occupied. We killed about 500 and captured about 5,000 before we got out of there. We lost many men.

We had set up our aid station in an old factory on a hill. Right next to the factory was a washhouse with lots of sinks where the factory workers could clean up. Alongside the washhouse was a little stone shed. Between the stone shed and the factory was a pretty wide driveway where we could get our jeeps in and out. Behind the factory was an open field with a stone wall around it.

I heard the fighting, so I got some binoculars and went to the stone wall to see what was going on. A tank shell fired over my head. The shell hit the little stone shed and made a sizable hole in it. It had to have come pretty close to my head to hit the shed. There were two vehicles parked by the shed and a couple of men, but no one got hurt, which was amazing considering how close and powerful the explosion was.

From the yard of our aid station way up on the hill we could see a castle made of red brick. It had four towers at each corner and one big tower on the front side, with many small spires in between. All day long our tank was shooting at the castle – "Boom, Boom, Boom!" Overnight they would leave the tank parked on the road.

Right next to the tank was a chicken house, so a couple of us went out one night to see if we could find any eggs. The guys that had been running the tank were standing around talking. We heard some bullets flying around us.

The tank driver said, "We had better get back inside the tank!"

My buddy and I decided we didn't want any eggs after all. We took off at a run back to the aid station.

The road that went by our aid station went down along the river. We got word that there were two wounded down around the curve where they were fighting. It was too dangerous to go down the road, where we would be under observation. Across the road there was a section of houses very close to each other. We decided to go from house to house down around to where they were fighting. When we got to the house closest to the fighting they told us it was too dangerous to go any further. They said to wait until nightfall, so we worked our way house to house back up to the aid station and waited.

That afternoon we saw something coming up the road from the direction of the fighting. It was a four-wheel trailer and both of the wounded men were on it. Two German women were pushing the trailer. They brought it up to the aid station. To thank the women we told them they could go back to where they came from, but they wanted to keep going.

Later that day a German woman came by carrying a baby. She went on down the road and shortly after that we heard an explosion. We found the mother and baby; an artillery shell had killed them both.

When the troops went into battle, we stayed as close behind

them as we could to see if there were any wounded. As we were waiting, another tank pulled up beside us. The driver spotted a dead German on the road. He hopped off the tank and went to check him out. He turned him over and saw a brand new camera. He took it, but I never would have. I didn't mess with the dead.

Shortly afterward we heard there was a wounded in the next town. As we were going to pick him up, we saw around 20 German civilians crossing an open field. The German soldiers were shooting at them. I don't know if they were trying to kill them, or just shooting over their heads as a warning. We found one wounded American and one wounded German. We had a rack on the back of the jeep, so we could carry two men.

We moved our aid station into town. Even though we could hear fighting a few blocks away, we felt safe enough to venture out. There was a small group of us from the medical attachment. We went into a vacant house and found a ham hanging in the back room. We decided to celebrate Easter Sunday in that house. We got out the best dishes and a clean tablecloth and set the table. The chaplain stopped by, so we invited him to eat with us. Our meal was interrupted when two American soldiers came by with a German soldier who had been hit in the hand. We put a bandage on his hand, they went on, and we finished our meal.

I don't remember the exact order of how they happened, but the following are some other stories from Aschaffenburg.

One time we saw an American lying out in a field. We thought he was wounded, so two of us went out to pick him up. When we got there we found out he was dead. We were being shot at, so we had to leave him. We took off at a run.

Another time the Germans had captured one of our tanks. The German tank and our tank were at a standoff about a block apart. We got the first shot off and it knocked the German tank out of commission.

One day we were bringing a wounded man back to the aid station on foot. An American soldier with two German prisoners passed us. He had them walking in front of him so he could keep an eye on them. They got to the corner before we did and stepped out into the street. One of our tanks was parked up the street and didn't realize they were prisoners. They shot them with a machine gun and killed them both.

Another time I was walking down the street and I saw a German officer hanging from a sign. The German major had hung himself because he wanted to give up.

We kept our aid station as close to the fighting as we could. We were about five blocks away. My buddy Ray and I were sitting outside the aid station and there wasn't much going on until a rifleman came running up and said there was a wounded guy up the street. Ray and I grabbed a stretcher and followed him.

We were running alongside a brick wall. The Germans were shooting at us. I saw a bullet hit the wall in front of the rifleman, and another bullet hit the wall between the rifleman and Ray, and one hit between Ray and me. I never looked to see if one hit behind me.

We just continued to run as fast as we could. After we ran about four blocks, we saw an American rifle and helmet lying in the street. We then saw an open doorway and ducked in. There were two men inside the building. One was a lieutenant and the other was our aid man attached to F Company.

I asked, "Where is the wounded man?"

They said he was in the building across the street. The wounded man was on the second floor, so we had to go back outside and up a set of stairs to get to him. I said that since I had been bringing up the rear, I would go first. The lieutenant said not to spend much time standing in the doorway and to go as fast as we could. When I got to the top of the stairway, they had the door open and I slid in. There were about five men in the room. Some of them were shooting out of the windows. I asked where the wounded man was.

He said, "I'm over here!"

I asked him how he was doing. He had been bandaged up and said he was doing pretty good.

I said, "Find a safe place out of the line of sight, and as soon as things have quieted down we will come back and get you."

I went over to the doorway to holler at Ray not to come across. Just as I got to the door Ray came sliding in. I looked back across the street. The rifleman that had been guiding us stepped into the doorway to come across, and he was shot right in the chest while I helplessly looked on. Ray and I hurried back across the street. When we got there the aid man was bandaging the rifleman up. The aid man said he was in pretty bad shape.

The lieutenant said, "There's no way out of here. There's no back door!"

I looked at Ray and he looked at me. We didn't say a word. I walked over to the front of the stretcher and Ray walked to the back, and out the door we went on a dead run. As far as I know, no one shot at us.

When we got back to the aid station, they asked us, "Where did you get him?"

We said, "Down the street."

We didn't find out whether he lived or died, but at least we gave him a chance. Ray and I were pretty tired out from carrying him five blocks at a dead run. Ray said he hadn't known whether he could keep up. I said that I was afraid to slow down or he might have run me over.

A few days later we ran into one of the soldiers from F Company. He said the lieutenant was putting us in for the Silver Star. The lieutenant said it was the bravest thing he had ever seen and he wouldn't have done it himself. He had put us in for the Silver Star, but he didn't know what our names were.

Ray and Walter Collins were the two small guys in our outfit, so they got them mixed up. I was average height. They confused me for my buddy Bill McDermott. The way I found this out was that Walter Collins later told me he was getting the Silver Star for something he did in Aschaffenburg, but he didn't remember doing it at all. He showed me a copy of the write-up and I realized what had happened. I talked to Ray and we decided to let it go and not make a big fuss about it. We were just doing our job. We thought, "What good is a medal?"

The next day the Germans surrendered and the battle of Aschaffenburg was over.

CHAPTER 20
On Toward Munich

When we left Aschaffenburg we headed for Bamberg, Germany. We thought it would be well defended, as it was a big industrial city. The 180th Battalion was going to come in from the left and our battalion, the 157th, was going to come in from the right. The 180th was well ahead of us because we were held up in Aschaffenburg.

In order for us to move faster, a task force was formed. It consisted of six tanks. The first was a lead tank, and the infantry rode on the next five tanks. The task force was to move ahead as quickly as possible. If they ran into too much resistance, they were to stop and stay where they were until the main force arrived. In doing this, it allowed the main force to move more quickly without running into an ambush.

Besides the six tanks there were two jeeps following along behind. One of them had the battalion commander, the jeep driver, and two litter bearers, including myself. We were moving quickly as we came up over a hill. There was a small town in the valley below. There was a fairly large field between us and where the Germans had dug in.

When the task force got there, the men got off the tanks and started down the hill toward the Germans. As they started down the hill, the German machine gun bullets were firing toward the infantry. One of our tanks turned around and silenced the machine guns by firing a shell that would spread apart and take out a lot of guns. It wasn't long before the Germans realized that they were outnumbered and decided to retreat.

One of the Germans got out of his foxhole and started running toward the town. He turned his head to look behind him. One of our infantrymen shot at the man and shot his nose right off his face without touching either cheek.

When someone asked me if we had killed him, I said, "No, but he never smelled very good after that."

After this man was shot, the Germans decided to surrender. They were escorted to the rear and to a prisoner of war camp. As all of this fighting was going on, we were sitting back on top of the hill in the jeep, and it seemed like we were watching a movie.

When the fighting stopped we drove on into town. It was a small town along a little stream. There were several buildings on fire. The local fire department was out fighting the fire. They were all old men and women. I was thinking that maybe all the young men were out fighting. We thought it was funny that they all had their fire hats and uniforms on. They had a hose that went into the stream and a pump they operated manually.

CHAPTER 21
Nuremberg

W hen the 180th Battalion got to Bamberg, they found out that the Germans had decided not to defend it. We figured that the 180th could clear out the Germans that were there and secure the town, so we headed on to Nuremberg (Nürnberg).

When we got to Nuremberg, our sector was stationed where the main train station used to be. Nuremberg was the main rail center, so it had been bombed quite heavily. There wasn't a building or wall standing for three blocks on either side. There were pieces of railroad tracks standing on end and pieces of trains. The main rail station was completely gone, but the big opera house nearby didn't look like it had been damaged at all.

It was a pretty open area where our troops were coming through. They hadn't gone very far when a soldier was wounded, so my litter squad went to get him. The company aid man was protecting the wounded guy behind the wheel of a train that had been blown up. The aid man said that when the man got hit he ran over to take care of him. The Germans shot a hole in the canteen that was fastened to his belt, but it didn't hit him at all.

The original city of Nuremberg had a moat around it that had been there for centuries. There was no longer any water in the moat, and there were trees growing out of it. Where the drawbridges used to be they built permanent bridges. The town had expanded out quite a ways from the original one.

Our first night there we heard that we had captured some Polish refugees that the Germans had been using as forced labor. My buddy and I decided to go down and see what was going on. There wasn't much happening, but we saw some fellows that we knew and stopped to talk to them. It was getting dark and I thought we should go back, but my buddy said he wanted to stay and talk a while.

I headed back by myself and I was doing fine until I asked someone if I was going in the right direction. He said no and pointed in what he thought was the right direction. Soon it was dark and I didn't have any idea where I was. To make things worse, I didn't have my steel helmet with me. I don't know why I didn't bring it. I usually had it with me at all times. I even slept with it. When it got dark the fighting started again. There was shooting all around. I went up one street and there was a tank parked there. I started to go around it and one of the tank guys asked me where I was going.

I said, "Down the street."

He said, "Don't go down there, that's where the Germans are."

So I started back up the sidewalk. There were a couple of soldiers coming down the sidewalk toward me. I could hear them talking. They got to the corner before I did. When they got to the cross street there were Germans coming up the side. They started shooting at each other, so I crossed the street and went up the other side. I was completely lost. All the buildings looked alike. In one place there was a dead German lying in the street. I know I passed him more than once, so I must have been going in a circle.

I said to myself, "Enough of this!"

I decided to go up the street one more time. If I couldn't find a way out I was going to hole up in one of the houses overnight. As I was walking up the street, one of the doors opened up. It was two guys coming out to look for me.

They had a large stadium in Nuremberg with a big swastika above it. Hitler had given speeches there from a marble and gold podium. It was where he started forming the Nazi party. In the early days, they were always parading around showing off. It was empty when we got there and the big swastika had been blown off the top.

We were there on Hitler's 56th (and last) birthday, April 20th. There were no Nazis celebrating in the stadium that day. Instead, we celebrated the complete victory of Nuremberg on that day. 2,600 prisoners had been taken. Throughout the whole battle, 10,000 had been taken. An estimated 1,300 Germans had been killed or wounded. The next day a formal flag raising ceremony was held at the stadium.

Everyone got ice cream. I heard they had discovered a building about the size of a whole city block that was full of frozen goods. Boy, were we happy to get that ice cream! I couldn't remember the last time I'd had ice cream. We left Nuremberg on April 22nd, 1945 and we were on the line until the end of the war.

Our next challenge was crossing the Danube River. When we got to the river the bridge had been blown out. The river was flooded, running full from bank to bank. Some of the men were disappointed when we got to the river. We had imagined it as a big blue river, and it looked more like a muddy creek.

I don't know where they got them, but some of the soldiers showed up with some 10-foot rowboats to get the men across. They could only carry six people at a time. It took all day to get them all across. They were being shot at all the while, and the men waiting on shore were right in the line of fire.

There were a bunch of guys waiting by the river to be rowed across. Our new battalion commander was down there checking the situation out. He was standing there with an aid man on one side and one of the officers on the other side when he was shot in the shoulder, but the other men didn't get a scratch on them.

The combat engineers wanted to rebuild the bridge as soon as possible. They tied a rope onto one of the boats and asked the guys to tie it on the other side so they could start working on the bridge, but something went wrong. The rope got caught up on something and it sank the boat. The guys swam ashore and just as they got into the shallow water a mortar shell exploded right where they were.

We had to go into the water to get them and take them back to the aid station, which was about a half mile up the road. We had to go back and forth between the aid station and the shore all day long. I don't remember how many trips we made, but the medics said they used more plasma that day than they had in a long time.

Meanwhile the combat engineers were working on the bridge. It was amazing what those engineers could build using just the materials they could find around them. They were using telephone poles and lumber from blown out buildings, and whatever else they could find. They put up a floodlight. With the light they had no cover, but they worked all night long and finished at about 10am the next morning.

We were in the second jeep to drive across the bridge, right after the company commander. There were five of us in the jeep, three in the front and two in the back. I was in the back, and the two of us were facing back. Looking over the side, I could see mortar shell hitting the ground alongside us. The jeep made a lot of noise, so we couldn't hear it, and the guys in the front couldn't see it. I turned my head to tell them about the shells when it felt like somebody hit me in the head with a baseball bat.

A mortar shell had landed just to the right of the jeep. It shredded the tire and punctured the radiator. The jeep driver managed to keep the jeep on the road. He drove on down the road until we saw a house. We stopped to check each other out and bandage each other up. There were five of us in the jeep and four of us were wounded. I got hit in the forehead, and had scratches on my eyelid and nose. The lieutenant sent another guy and myself on down the road so they could radio back and warn any other vehicles that were coming up.

That night my back was hurting so I had a medic look at it. He said there were several small pieces of shrapnel in my back, but they were too small to remove. They were still in there when I got home. They could still be there as far as I know.

CHAPTER 22

My Last Days in the War

Living On Borrowed Time

We moved around a lot. After the war I'd look at a map of France and sometimes I wasn't anywhere near where I thought I'd been. The Germans were good at retreating. You'd be fighting and not move an inch, and then all of a sudden they'd retreat and be gone.

After we crossed the Danube River, the Germans were retreating very quickly. F Company decided to push off at 4am the next morning. This was to keep the Germans retreating so they wouldn't have time to dig in anywhere. They wanted litter bearers with them, so two of us along with a jeep driver followed behind the troops.

It was cold at 4am in the morning. The sky was so clear that we could see every star. After a couple of hours, F Company had advanced quite a ways, and had run into no opposition. We got a messenger from up front who told us that a vehicle had broken down. They told us it would be an hour to an hour and a half before we moved on.

The jeep driver said, "I saw a little town back a ways, let's go back and make some coffee."

We always carried a tin of coffee with us. We went back and stopped at the first house in the town. We parked our jeep under a little shed by the back door. We knocked on the door and woke up an older couple that had obviously been asleep. Boy, were they surprised to see us! We asked the woman if she had any eggs. We had learned the German word for eggs soon after we arrived in Germany. She said she did, so we fired up the wood stove and put a pot on for coffee while she got the eggs to cooking.

The jeep driver went out to get the coffee from the jeep. I heard him talking to someone. I was quite surprised when the F Company commanding officer came walking in.

The Commander said, "You sure are a rugged bunch of individuals. I brought my men to get the Germans out of town and you're in here having breakfast."

The old German couple probably had some stories to tell their grandchildren. We were likely the first Americans they had seen. I don't remember if we got to finish our breakfast before we moved on. I don't remember what happened the rest of that day.

The next thing I remember, we were walking down the road toward Munich in a column of twos. The road was built up about 3½ feet. We hadn't run into any resistance. Up ahead of us a ways off to the right was a little group of trees. As the road got closer to the wooded area the Germans started shooting at us with machine guns, so we ducked down into the ravine by the side of the road where they couldn't hit us. We could crawl along behind the road and be pretty well protected.

As we advanced we came to a crossroad and we had no protection crossing that. We tried running across one at a time. The riflemen were trying to cover for us, but they needed to get across too. The lieutenant decided it would be faster and safer if he called for more artillery. He called for the radioman to come up to where he was. The radio was quite large, so the radioman had it strapped onto his back.

Just as he got to me, he said, "I hate these radios, you can't get down low enough."

Right then, the radioman was shot through the head and he fell down right on top of me. Another soldier took the radio off his back and took it up to the lieutenant.

Shortly after that the artillery shells started coming in. When shooting an artillery gun, the shooter can't see where they are shooting. Another person is needed to observe where the shells land and then tell the artillery shooter to increase his turns right or left, or increase the range. The shells were going off over our heads. Nobody waited for the lieutenant to give directions to increase the range. Everybody got up and took off on the run for some houses to take cover in. After the artillery drove the Germans out we went on down the road.

The 2nd Battalion was to take over the airport at Munich. We looked down on the airport from the high ground. We could see people running around and some small fires. We could see that the Germans were not trying to protect the airport, so we decided to pass on by and head for the city of Munich.

The 3rd Battalion, which was on our left, seized the Dachau prison camp and freed its 32,000 prisoners. When they pulled into Dachau, they saw 40 boxcars full of prisoners, some dead and some alive. The Germans had intended to move them, but didn't have time. They were going to destroy the evidence, but we got there before they could

Both sides of the tracks were littered with dead bodies. There were bodies stacked everywhere. They could see that some of them had tried to escape but didn't make it beyond the tracks. I heard horror stories beyond comprehension. I was sure glad I wasn't involved in that.

That night our battalion, the 2nd, stayed on the outskirts of Munich, just a short way from Dachau's prison camp. I slept in a house that belonged to one of the guards at the prison camp. I found a pocket watch that had belonged to him. I took it as a souvenir. I figured he wouldn't have any use for it now.

On May 2nd, 1945 we moved into Munich. On the first night we stayed close to a tavern where the Americans had tried to kill Hitler once. We thought we would stay in Munich for a while and then push on up to the Alps where Hitler's retreat was. There were rumors that the Germans were going to fight to the last man.

Immediately after we moved into Munich the 45th Division took over the radio station. We got to hear all the latest news. Before we had a chance to move on we heard that the war was over! There was no big celebration, just a sigh of relief. It took a while for it to sink in.

We stayed in Munich until the middle of June. The whole medical attachment of 32 men moved into a big apartment house on the corner of Elizabeth and King Street. We had the aid station on the first floor, and the litter bearers and aid men got the whole second floor. It was great! We had beds to sleep in, and a bathroom with hot water and electric lights. It was the first time I got to have a bath since I had left home.

The 2nd Battalion took over the post office and set up their headquarters and a kitchen where we went for all of our meals. There was also a place where they showed movies. One of the guys asked another if he wanted to go with him to the movies.

The second guy said, "No, I went last night, and it was cold and the roof leaked."

The first guy replied, "I have been cold and wet a lot this past year and I didn't get to see a movie."

In the town there was a swimming pool. I didn't get to go, but the guys who didn't have a rank got to go and pass out suits and towels there, and were able to swim. The guys that did have a rank had to stay back and work. I was a T5 (Tech 5) ranking.

We didn't have much to do, so we spent a lot of time just walking around town. One day my buddy and I were walking by the post office where the mess hall was. One of the cooks was crossing the street when a .50 caliber machine gun bullet fell out of the air and hit his hand and tore a chunk out of the back of it. We hadn't heard any gunfire so we didn't know where it had come from. It could have been someone cleaning out their gun miles away.

Another time while we were out walking we saw a plane in the air going straight down. It crashed, bursting into a ball of fire. We never did find out what had happened to it.

Somebody in the aid station noticed that I was limping and asked me what the problem was.

I said, "Oh, just my ankle that I hurt back in October."

They said it looked quite swollen and I had better go over to the hospital and get it x-rayed. They took me over in a jeep. After they x-rayed it the medical officer came in and told me I had a very bad break in my ankle.

I asked him, "What do you do for that?"

His reply was, "Stay off of it for a few days."

I had been walking on it for 10 months.

In order to get back where I had been, I had to go to the replacement depot. There we waited until they had enough men to fill a truck, then they'd take us back to Munich. While there, I had a close call. I almost got stuck on KP (kitchen patrol) duty. A medic from another outfit said he couldn't go on guard duty because he was a medic and medics were not allowed to carry guns, so instead they put him on KP. KP stands for "keep peeling." Kitchen helpers might have to peel potatoes or scrub floors. That night when I was supposed to go on guard duty I told the sergeant I was a medic, so he told me to go back to the tent and I got out of both duties. I was lucky. I got to go back to Munich before it was time to do KP again.

While I was gone the guys got a great big bottle of wine and a big block of cheese. I tried it, but it was a too potent for me. They spent much of the time drinking wine and eating cheese. One night one of the guys had a bit too much to drink and was chasing his best buddy with a knife. Another guy had a little .25 caliber revolver, which was small enough to hold in the palm of his hand. He was so drunk that he accidentally shot himself in the finger. He was upset because they would think he shot himself on purpose to get out of the service. He would be court marshaled! He didn't do much damage to his hand. The gun was so small that the bullet was just stuck underneath the skin on his finger, so nothing ever came of it.

CHAPTER 23
The Post-War Weeks

There were all kinds of rumors. One was that the 45th Division was going to Japan. Points were awarded for how long each person had been in the army, how many dependents they had, for every medal received and others for things I can't remember. The high point men like me were transferred out and the low point men from other outfits were transferred in to take our places. They tried to talk us into staying with the division, but I thought doing occupational duty for the time required would be better than getting shot getting off a boat in Japan. I could have been a regimental clerk if I'd stayed with the division. I had no idea what that was, but I just wanted to go home.

I said, "No way!"

I was transferred to the 103rd Division, which was doing occupational duty up in the Austrian mountains. We got on the train at Munich at about 1pm in the afternoon headed for Innsbruck, Austria. From there we were to be transferred by truck up to the little town of Obergurgl. The entire trip was supposed to take about four hours. We'd been on the train about two hours when they realized we were going in the wrong direction. They backed the train clear back to Munich, turned the train around and headed in the right direction.

We didn't get into Innsbruck until about 4pm. One of the

nicest parts of the trip was when we went through the foothills of the Alps as the sun was setting. The last seven miles of the road going up to Obergurgl was one-way traffic. They had a phone set up so we could call ahead, as there was no place for a truck to let another vehicle pass or turn around.

Obergurgl was a little resort town for skiers. There was a big ski lodge with 500 pairs of skis, which was only open for about four months out of the year. Obergurgl has the highest elevation of any town in Austria. We got to stay in a nice hotel. I had a room all to myself. It was very comfortable and had two big feather beds. It was pretty dull. I didn't know anybody. Nobody asked me who I was or told me what I was supposed to do.

It was a small town. We could spit from one side to the other. The only thing to see was a guy cutting hay along the side of the hill with a sickle. We had a few snowflakes on the 4th of July. I was only there two or three weeks, but it was the most boring time of the whole war. After that I was transferred back to Nuremberg with the 1st Division, who were doing MP duty at the war trials.

CHAPTER 24
Back to Nuremberg

I got into Nuremberg late at night and they showed me to a bunk where I was supposed to sleep. When I got ready to go to bed I hung my camera on the bedpost. There was nowhere else to put it. When I woke up in the morning, it was gone. I found out some of the men sleeping in the same area had gone to Paris on a pass. I hope they got some good pictures.

Our aid station was right across the street from where they were having the war trials. The men who were doing MP duty at the trials wore their dress uniforms and white helmets. I saw them bringing war criminals in, but I never got to go into the courthouse. I saw them bringing in Hermann Göring, a big military leader of the Nazi Party. He was sentenced to death, but he committed suicide by taking cyanide the night before he was going to be hanged.

This time while we were in Nuremberg we got to stay at the Grand Hotel. Nuremberg had been very heavily bombed. Just a little ways from the Grand Hotel was where the train station used to be. The Grand Hotel was used as a rest stop for men who had gone out on a pass to England or Paris and couldn't get back to their outfits.

We had a temporary aid station there in case someone needed minor attention. We never had any patients the whole time we were there. My buddy and I ate our meals at the hotel's restaurant. We could order off the menu and eat anything we wanted for free. I never had to pay anything to go on the streetcars either. I just got on and off as I pleased.

They wanted to keep track of everyone while the war trials were going on, so everyone had to have a pass everywhere they went. They brought us a pass every day. One day I wanted to leave and I hadn't gotten my pass yet. A truck with two MPs stopped me. Two colored guys were also stopped. The MP asked if I had a pass. I showed him yesterday's pass; he smiled and let me go. The two colored men, however, were hauled off.

One night they brought a colonel in who didn't have a pass. He was very upset and disturbed that he had been picked up. The captain told him that everyone had to have a pass, no matter who they were, day or night. He kept saying that he was a colonel and he had a pass back where he was staying.

The captain said, "Ok, I'll let you go, but I want you back in here by 10am tomorrow morning with your pass. If you don't show up, I'll send someone out to pick you up again."

Nothing had been going on at the Grand Hotel so they sent me to a barracks right in the middle of the city where the MPs from the trials were staying. One night in the middle of the night, a guy came in from guard duty with a big cut on his head. I asked him how he got it and he mumbled something I couldn't hear. The next day I found out what had happened. He had come in from guard duty and was making a lot of noise. Someone told him to shut up, but he didn't.

The guy said, "If you don't shut up, I'm going to hit you in the head with this bottle!"

He said, "You wouldn't dare!"

He dared.

We always called the African Americans "colored guys." A lot of them worked at a big supply depot on the edge of Nuremberg. They worked there but were stationed in Nuremberg. One night they decided to have a dance and invited a bunch of German girls. There was a curfew. Everyone had to be off the street by a certain time of night. It was close to curfew, but the dance was still going strong. A couple of the MPs where I was staying decided to go check it out.

By the time they got there it was past curfew. They told the German women it was time to go home and the colored guys to get back to their barracks. The colored guys weren't very happy about it. The MPs were glad they made it out of there in one piece.

Everything was segregated. The colored guys decided to take over a little German town and got the word out that no white soldier should be in there after dark. It wasn't too smart to say that to men who had just been out at the front fighting for months. The MPs loaded up a couple of men and headed out there one evening. I grabbed my first aid kit and went along.

They stopped the trucks at the edge of the town and all the MPs spread out in just the same way as they had taken towns during the war. The colored guys had a German machine gun. They fired a couple of bursts over our heads. When we got into the town, there was a machine gun and some other weapons, but not a person to be found.

Since there wasn't much for us to do in Nuremberg, I was sent out to a little town at the edge of the city called Fürth. The day after I got there I got into a strange situation. There were three of us medics, and one got a pass to go to England. The other medic was chauffeuring a colonel at the war trials, so that left me to take care of any sick or injured in our company.

No one told me what to do. I got up when I wanted to in the mornings. I had coffee and doughnuts for breakfast and took a shower. I went down to the Red Cross. I made sure I got back to the company in time for dinner. Right after dinner I was in charge of sick call, where patients would come in to be looked at. I remember one guy having a big, nasty looking boil. I had to drain it, put medicine on it and bandage it up. After sick call I was pretty much on my own.

Sometimes I would take the streetcar into Nuremberg and go swimming in the pool where the 1936 Olympics had been held. One day they were having a USO show in a big opera house and I went to that. It was like a vaudeville show. There was a comedian, a magician, acrobats, singers and dancers in skimpy costumes. I remember it being very entertaining.

CHAPTER 25
Time to Go Home

My last few weeks in Nuremberg were very uneventful. I remember reading in The Stars and Stripes newspaper about the nuclear bomb dropped on Hiroshima. Shortly after that it was declared that the Japanese had surrendered.

Right after that I was told I had enough points to go home. I was transferred to the 9th Armored Division and I would go home with them. I figured it was about time. The 9th Armored was located up by the Czechoslovakian border. It wasn't too long after I joined them that we were sent to Marseille, France to catch a ship to go home. They sent us by train, but it wasn't a passenger train, just boxcars.

Whenever we stopped for a break the French men wanted to buy cigarettes, clothing or whatever else they could get from us. Two of the soldiers were working together. One of them would sell a carton of cigarettes for $20. As soon as the deal was complete, the other soldier would show up with an MP armband and demand that the cigarettes be handed over. He would make quite a show of scolding the purchaser and tell him not to do it again. They did this every time we stopped.

The captain came back after one stop wearing just his undershirt. He laughed and said it was the first time he'd ever sold the shirt off his back. I was upset because I had left behind an entire duffel bag of clothes that I didn't want to carry back on the train. I could have been a rich man!

The captain had a typewriter he was going to bring home, but he got a little worried about the fact that it had a sticker that said "US Medical Core" on it. I was able to remove the sticker and took it all the way home with me.

The men were allowed to take home guns or any other souvenirs they wanted to as long as it was okay with their commanding officer. I brought home two guns, some watches (one belonging to the guard at the Dachau prison camp), a German flag, some German medals and other miscellaneous items.

Just out of Marseille we got word that the ship we were supposed to be on was delayed, so they sent us to a camp about 20 miles from Paris to wait until the ship arrived. We could go into Paris for the day, but the truck that left for Paris left at 4am in the morning, and that was too early for me. One of the guys who went to Paris got drunk and missed the truck going back to camp. A couple of French women took him in. They fed him and gave him a place to sleep. He sobered up and caught the next truck back to camp.

Finally we got word that we could continue our journey. The train this time was a regular passenger train. It had compartments that held four people, but they put six of us in a compartment, so it was a little crowded. They told us our ship had arrived, but a propeller had been damaged coming into the harbor. They had to get it fixed, so it was another week before we could go home.

They sent us to a camp up on a hill overlooking the Mediterranean Sea. The wind blew all the time. The roads were dusty, so everyone's clothes had dust all over them. Some smart guy decided that if he put oil on the roads that would keep the dust down. Instead of having regular dust, we had oily dust.

I didn't have any regular duties, but I had to help out with first aid once in a while. A whole bunch of guys came down with shingles. We found a sprayer used for spraying flies. We filled it with the medicine and sprayed the guys with it. It eased the itching.

Our ship finally arrived. It was the second largest passenger ship the United States owned. During peacetime the ship was called the SS Washington. In wartime, it was the USS Mt Vernon. They put 4,000 troops on board. I don't know how big the crew was, but it must have been pretty large as well.

We sailed on October 4th, 1945. As we were leaving the shore we saw a large group of porpoise following the ship. Due to the large amount of men on the ship, they only fed us two meals a day. By the time they were finished with one meal it was time to start in on the next. I got stuck on KP. Once when I was done with my shift one of the crew brought down a case of Coke.

There wasn't much to do on the ship, but they had a speaker set up so we could hear the World Series being broadcast on the radio. On Columbus Day, October 12th, 1945, I arrived back in Norfolk to the same port I had left from. When we pulled into port there was a band playing for us. We were taken back to nearby Camp Patrick Henry.

CHAPTER 26
Back in the States

It was good to be back in the states after 21 months overseas. It took us 21 days to get overseas, but only 8 to get home. This was because going over we had a convoy of 56 ships and the convoy could only go as fast as the slowest ship.

In the Army there are two good meals – the one right before leaving and the one right after getting home. I don't remember what we had to eat, but they had a cold milk machine with all the milk we could drink. Boy did that taste good after not having had any for such a long time.

We had to wait a week before we could get a train going to the west coast. There were 12 in our group headed for Fort Lewis, Washington. We got to Fort Lewis on a Friday, and they weren't doing any processing until Monday, so my buddy and I hitched a ride to Portland for the weekend.

When I got into Portland, I called my folks but they weren't home, so I called my Uncle Gene and he came to pick us up. I don't remember much about that, but I do remember going to church. I went to church to see my friends that I used to hang around with, but most of the kids had moved or gone to college. My folks had moved into a different house while I was gone. It was a bigger house. It had three floors and my room was on the top floor.

I was supposed to be back up to Fort Lewis by noon on

Monday to get my discharge papers. I got up early and took the 7am bus thinking I'd have plenty of time to get there by noon. It didn't work out that way. The bus stopped in every little town and we didn't get up there until 1pm. That was the only time in the service that I was AWOL and it was to get my discharge. I didn't miss much, just the speech they gave us to reenlist or join the reserves.

Before we went home they issued us new clothing. While I was waiting in line I noticed another soldier that I had taken my training with. One reason I remembered him was that when I had originally arrived at Fort Lewis they had issued us new clothing, and he was in line with a shirt of one kind and a pair of trousers of another. Believe it or not, here we were after 27 months and he was again being issued a shirt of one kind and a pair of pants of another.

They gave us new clothes, $300 and our discharge papers. Just like that I was a civilian again. When I was discharged, I thought I was going to go home and pick right back up where I left off, but it doesn't happen that way. Things change.

CHAPTER 27
Job Hunting

After resting up for a few weeks, I decided I should think about getting a job. Before I left the newspaper had been full of ads for jobs, but during the war a lot of people had come to Portland to work in the shipyards and on other wartime jobs. A lot of them stayed and continued to take up those jobs.

The government had a program called 5220. They would give me $20 a week for 52 weeks while I was looking for work. I went all over town looking for jobs. While I was out looking for work a lot of places wouldn't take my resume because I wasn't 21. I was only 20 years old when I was discharged. It was frustrating because I was old enough to fight, but not old enough to vote or work. At the time the voting age was 21.

I had to report to the unemployment office once a week to get my $20. One week when I was at the unemployment office, they said they wanted to see me in the office. The man asked me why I had turned down a job the week before. The job paid $26 for six days of work. I told him I couldn't live on that.

He said, "Can you live on $20 a week?"

I said, "No, but that is supposed to help me until I can get a job that is more than $26 for six days. Would you take a job where you would only get $6 more and tie you up so you couldn't look for a real job?"

He said, "No," and let me go back to job hunting.

One of the problems was that I didn't have a high school diploma. I was drafted right after my junior year. I went to the school and asked what I needed to do to get my diploma. They told me I needed five credits. I could come back to school from October to November or go and take a series of tests. I took four tests. I got over 90% on each test. Some were on things I hadn't even studied in school. I was surprised I passed with flying colors! I hadn't even thought about school for 27 months.

One week when I went down to the unemployment office they had a job for me at the airport checking baggage. To take the bus I had to go across town about four miles, then transfer to a bus going near the airport. It didn't go all the way, so I had to go into a little tavern and call for a shuttle to the airport.

The airport didn't have a terminal like it does now. At about the middle of the airport on the Columbia River side there were two buildings. One was United, where I worked, and the other was Northwest. They had a kitchen where they prepared the food that was put on the planes. Any food that didn't get eaten was sent back to the kitchen and we got to eat it. They said employees at the airport could get a free ride up to Seattle and back, but I never went.

My job was as a baggage checker. When people came in we checked their baggage for them and gave them a receipt. We didn't have to load it onto the planes; another crew did that. When a plane came in, a stairway was rolled over for the people to get out. Next they came to us. We took their receipts and gave them their luggage. Sometimes we got a tip and sometimes we didn't.

We worked two weeks on day shift, two weeks on night shift, and then on the relief shift, which could be day or night. We worked five days a week, but we never got Saturday or Sunday off. The job paid $150 per month, which wasn't good wages at the time. The next best job was selling tickets. It paid the same but an applicant had to have a year of college to get it.

There was a spot for limousines to pull up. One night there was a very bad storm and one was parked on the flat street beside the terminal. It took off, being blown down the street. There were a couple of planes parked on the runway and they had them parked into the wind to keep them from blowing away.

On the other side of the airport where the Air Force base was, a small bi-plane was up flying, and every time it tried to land, the wind would force it up again. Finally about a dozen guys jumped up and grabbed the plane and pulled it down. It wasn't very heavy because it had cloth wings instead of metal.

After working there a couple of months I got tired of never getting Sundays off to go to church. I asked if there was a chance I could get some Sundays off.

They said, "NO."

I quit. I can still brag about having worked for United Airlines, but I don't tell people what I did.

Before I went into the service, I had worked in a sheet metal shop in the shipyards. One day the unemployment office got a call that they needed someone, so they sent me out there.

Most of our work was simple, like after something had been welded we would polish it up. Me and one other guy had a job to polish a pea trough. It was a long rectangle that was on a slant. It had different sized holes for the different sized peas to pass through. We were using polish that came in a good-sized can. We had to go outside when a delivery truck backed up and ran over it. Polish squirted everywhere. We thought it was funny at the time, but when the boss heard about it, he didn't think it was funny and fired us both.

Before I looked for another job, my twin sister Betty and I decided to take a trip back to Kansas to visit our grandparents.

CHAPTER 28
Going Back to Kansas

We took the Greyhound bus from Portland to Dodge City, Kansas. When we got to Dodge City, our Uncle Seth picked us up and drove us to Jetmore where we stayed with our Grandpa and Grandma.

School wasn't out yet, so we went to the high school graduation. Two of my friends who I had gone to school with were also drafted before they were finished with high school, and had come home to finish and graduate. After the graduation they had a dance, and we stayed to visit a few people we knew, but no one asked Betty or I to dance.

The next day I went to visit Henry Whipple. Henry didn't go into the service because he had a bad leg. He started apologizing to me about not having gone into the service. I told him there was no need to apologize, that he would have gone if he'd been drafted. I didn't voluntarily sign up either.

When I was growing up in Kansas, there was one colored kid in our class named Nelson Moore. We didn't think of him as being colored. He was just one of the boys, and one of my very good friends. Henry, Nelson and I went everywhere together. I asked how Nelson was. Henry told me that Nelson had come back from the war a very bitter man. He was a black man, and didn't know what discrimination was until he'd gone into the service. Nelson had moved to Denver, Colorado. I learned later that he had died of cancer.

There was another boy named Charles Lomberg. He was also one of my good friends from school. Betty and I had only planned on staying a week, but Charles was in college and didn't return for another week, so I stayed and Betty went home.

Charles was very talented. He played piano and tuba. He could dance and sing, and wasn't a bit shy about doing it. He was in all the class plays. Someone once asked me how we came to be friends and I said he played the tuba, and I was the only friend of his big enough to carry it. Haha!

I had a nice visit with Charles, but it was time to head home. It was sad to leave my grandparents. It was another five years before I saw them again.

I sat on the bus with another guy about my age that was going out to Oregon to visit a girl he had met in the service. About a mile past Caldwell, Idaho, our bus had a flat tire. We weren't scheduled to stop there, but the bus driver had to get the tire fixed. He said it would take about an hour, so if we wanted to, we would have time to get a bite to eat. We went to a small diner nearby.

After we were seated the waitress came up to my friend and said, "You're from Medicine Hat, Kansas, aren't you?"

He said, "How do you know that?"

"You are coming here to visit one of my girlfriends."

We hadn't even been scheduled to stop there and his girl-friend was in Oregon. He couldn't think of anyone from his hometown that looked enough like him to make her think that.

He got off the bus in Central Oregon and I went on to Portland to look for a job. I never saw him again.

CHAPTER 29
Back in Portland

When I got back to Portland I got a job working in a warehouse for Libby, McNeil and Libby Cannery. They canned pears and pickles.

While I was working there I met a nice girl at church. I had known her brother before I was in the Army. After dating for about a year we decided to get married since I had a steady job. She had a job teaching school.

While I was working at Libby's I got a chance to start a job as an apprentice electrician. I worked at that job for 39 years before I retired.

Jeanne and I were married for 53 years before she passed away and had three children, one son and two daughters.

After 21 months in the service I had thought I could take up right where I left off, but things had changed. After having so many close calls, I felt like I was living on borrowed time after the service. I've had a few close calls since then, and people say I've been lucky, but I think it was God more than luck that sealed my fate.

GALLERY

These are some of the German souvenirs I picked up.

Here are some of the commendations I received.

I received three purple hearts for heroic service.

This is my combat infantry badge.

I was awarded the bronze star for heroic achievement.

An award I received for good conduct.

A unit citation that was given to the entire 2nd Battalion.

Each yellow line on this patch signifies 6 months in service.

I had an "Eager for Duty" pin for each shoulder.

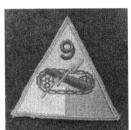

A patch signifying the 9th Armored Division.

A patch signifying the 45th Infantry Division.

The arrowhead signifies invasion, the stars are for each area of combat.

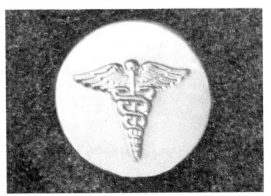

This is my medical insignia.

A small heater we used for cooking.

A War Ration Book.

Propaganda written by the Germans. Germans would shoot these out of a cannon to disperse them.

Me in the middle, by a church in France.

Litter bearers and aid men.

Litter bearers.

By the pillboxes on The Siegfried Line.

I am in the middle, transporting one German and two Americans to the aid station.

Living On Borrowed Time 164

A SELECTION OF LETTERS

Bill and his twin sister, Betty, who he wrote many of the following letters to.

V-Mail Service provides the most expeditious dispatch and reduces the weight of mail to and from personnel of our Armed Forces outside the continental United States. When addressed to points where micro-film equipment is operated, a miniature photographic negative of the message will be made and sent by the most expeditious transportation available for reproduction and delivery. The original message will be destroyed after the reproduction has been delivered. Messages addressed to or from points where micro-film equipment is not operated will be transmitted in their original form by the most expeditious means available.

INSTRUCTIONS

(1) Write the entire message plainly on the other side within marginal lines.

(2) PRINT the name and address in the two panels provided. Addresses to members of the Armed Forces should include rank or rating of the addressee, unit to which attached, and APO or Naval address.

(3) Fold, seal, and deposit in any post-office letter drop or street letter box.

(4) Enclosures must not be placed in this envelope and a separate V-Mail letter must be sent if you desire to write more than one sheet.

(5) V-Mail letters may be sent free of postage by members of the Armed Forces. When sent by others, postage must be prepaid at domestic rates (3c ordinary mail, 6c if air mail is desired).

☆ GPO 16—25143-2

Dear folks,

We started our training and I ready to quit. It is now 7:30 and I just got off work. First we had an hour of physical training Which wasn't good. Then we went to see a show on Military training, that wasn't bad. Then we had two hours where the told us how to take a rifle apart, & the name of all the parts. Now we are suported to know everything about a rifle, nuts.

Then then after noon they showed us how to make a pack. Then after that we went out in the field & marched. Most of the time the Louie spent bawling us out.

We had the best meal we have had yet this eve. We had beans. All we wanted. Then right after chow we had a fire drill. Then we had to go watch a ballgame whether we wanted to or not. And in about 30 min. We have to go to a show. This is a hell of a life.

We are on the move all day with out a minute to spare.

It is really hot here. And there is only one small fountain where ± 50 men have to drink.

Well I've got to run again

as never.

Bill.

P.S. If I don't get time to write don't be surprised.

I'll try to write as often as possible

Mon. Oct. 11, 43.

To whom it may concern.

Boy, I have really been busy
this eve. We pull out for Millers hill at
6:15 in the morning. We will be out there
for two days, so you probabl won't hear
from me.

You have probabl seen soldiers run a
obstil course in the shows. You know the part
where they swing acros the water on a
rope. Well, we have one like that. We
ran it this morning. There were only
two guys that fell in. Seargent Wallins
was one of them.

I can't tak any snapshots with out
something to tak them with.

Tell Pop he is better off when he
is and can do a lot more good.

We started studying the L. M. G. (light machine gun) today.

I got two letters from you today & two from Larry.

We had an inspection today. I passed OK. We had to turn in our dogtags to day so I guess they ain't planning on killing us off right away.

As ever

Bill
Wilson

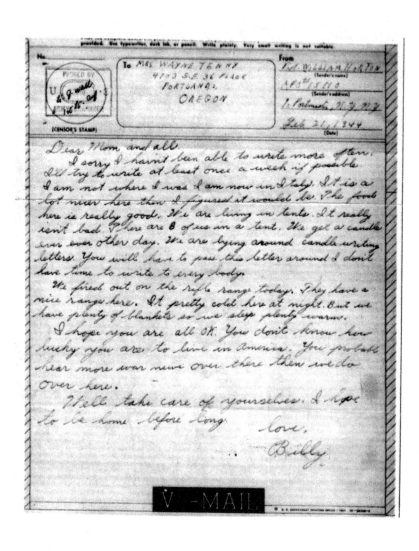

To MRS. WAYNE JENNY
4703 S.E. 36 PLACE
PORTLAND,
OREGON

From Pvt. WILLIAM HORTON
(Sender's name)
APO #15140
(Sender's address)
C Palmah, N. J. N. Y.
Feb 21, 1944
(Date)

[CENSOR'S STAMP]

PASSED BY
U
ARMY EXAMINER

Dear Mom and all,

I sorry I haint been able to write more often. I'll try to write at least once a week if possible. I am not where I was I am now in Italy. It is a lot nicer here then I figured it would be. The food here is really good. We are living in tents. It really isn't bad. There are 8 of us in a tent. We get a candle ever ever other day. We are lying around candle writing letters. You will have to pass this letter around I don't have time to write to every body.

We fired out on the rifle range today. They have a nice range here. It pretty cold here at night. But we have plenty of blankets so we sleep plenty warm.

I hope you are all OK. You don't know how lucky you are to live in America. You probably hear more war news over there then we do over here.

Well take care of yourselves. I hope to be home before long.

love,
Billy

No.____

To MISS BETTY HORTON
4703 S.E. 36 PLACE
PORTLAND,
OREGON

[CENSOR'S STAMP]

ARMY EXAMINER

From
Pvt. Wm. HORTON 39,336,32⅛
(Sender's name)
Med Det. 157ᵗʰ INF.
(Sender's address)
APO ⁿᵒ 45 %P.M., N.Y., N.Y.

MARCH 17, 1944
(Date)

Dear Sis and all,

Well everything is about the same except for a few
minor changes. We really have a nice hole to sleep
in now. With big logs over the top. We have trees,
grass, and flowers, growing all around us. The flowers
are violets. There is a spring less then 50 yds
from here so we have plenty of water.

For breakfast this morning I had a "K" ration
which consists of a three onz. can of chopped ham
and eggs, a few dog biscuits, a fruit bar, and a cup
of coffee which I made myself. Dinner is just
about the same except we have cheese instead of
meat, and lemon ade instead of coffee. And dextrose
tablets in the place of the fruit bar. For supper we
have pork for meat, chocolate bar for dessert, and bullion
to drink. Its the same old stuff everyday. at
least a guy never has to wonder what he is
going to have the next meal. I'm getting along
fine take care of yourself.

love,
Bill

V···MAIL

☆ U. S. GOVERNMENT PRINTING OFFICE I 1943   16—98262-4

No._____

PASSED BY
U.S. ARMY
EXAMINER

(CENSOR'S STAMP)

To MISS BETTY HORTON
4703 S.E. 36 PL.
PORTLAND, 2.
OREGON.

From
Pfc. WM. HORTON. 39,336,341
(Sender's name)
Med. Det. 1st InF.
(Sender's address)
APO 45 % P.M. N.Y, N.Y.
(Date)
AUG, 31, 1944

Dear Sis & all,

Well, here I am again, and doing fine, even if I do say so myself. Yesterday was a big day for me. I got a new suit of clothes & a bath. Both are few & far between. We went down to a small creek to bath. The other day I jumped in the river & then crawled on the ground on my tummy, so I really needed the clean clothes. France is really a beautiful country. We had a little shower last night, so everything is nice & fresh this morn. (even me). I am now setting on a pile of hay in a barn. There are a few geese, & chickens running around. You can forget about sending me anything for Christmas. There is nothing I need. And I have no way of taking care of anything. Besides I still plan to be home for Christmas.

Love & Kisses
Bill

V····MAIL

☆ U. S. GOVERNMENT PRINTING OFFICE 1943 10—28143-4

Sept. 11, 1944

Dear Folks,

Well, I guess I owe you a letter, since I received quite a few from you yesterday. There really isn't much to write about, nothing ever happen around here.

I got Linda picture all right. I got it when we were down by Salerno.

We went through a little town yesterday & the people gave us a lot of eggs & some bread. The people over here sure treat us swell. We had quite a little rain last week. We have been pretty lucky in getting a barn to sleep in lately. I just about fell out of a hay loft this morning.

I was talking to a German yesterday. He said, "Why for we fight I do not know." Then he went on to say that he thought Germany had lost the war etc.

Most of the Prisoners I've seen over here don't look much like supermen.

Well, there, isn't much more to say so I'll quit. send another package if you want to.

Love & Kisses

Bill

No._____

PASSED BY
U.S. ARMY EXAMINER
(CENSOR'S STAMP)

To MISS BETTY HORTON
4703 S.E. 36 PL.
PORTLAND,
OREGON

From Pvt. Wm Horton, 393832
(Sender's name)
Med. Det. 157 Inf.
(Sender's address)
APO 45 ℅ P.M. N.Y.N.

Oct. 8, 1944.
(Date)

Dear Sis + all,

I just got a package of fudge from you tonight. It's pretty darn good. Chester has been waiting for you to send some more. He is happy now. I fixed myself up this afternoon so I won't have to work for a while. I sprained my ankle playing ball. It is swollen up like a baloon. Today is Sunday, but we didn't have church. — To many of the boys are busy praying. It was really a lovely sun shining day. today. I was on K.P. today. But there isn't much to it. Well, I'll have to quit now. Chester wants to play cards. He is quite a nuisance.

Love, 1 Kiss
Billy

V --- MAIL

POST OFFICE DEPT. PCR

Feb. 5, 1945
France.

Dear Betty & all,

I have here before me 3 V mail letters from you & one from Mom that I have neglected to answer.

I was very fortunate in getting to go to a USO show this morning. There were 2 of us out of the medics that got to go. They took us back in trucks. It was quite a trip. It rained most of the way coming and going. But the show was really good, well worth the trip.

I think that's a good idea about getting a bigger place.

I also think it would be swell if Ivan could go out there too. If he wants to come but hasn't the money send him some of mine. I can't think of any better way to spend it.

I got a letter from aunt Lois the other day, but I haven't answered it yet.

I got to go to church yesterday. It is really a privilege to do so over here.

We don't have quite as nice a place to stay now. I is staying in a basement. It nice & warm & dry. There is a stove in it. We fry us up some yank last night. They were pretty darn good, I fried them my self.

Betty, don't feel bad about building the fire wrong. I tried to build one yesterday, and the old man up stairs finally had to build it for me.

Well, I haven't much to say except I sure wish I was home so I wouldn't have to write so many letters.

Well, don't work to hard, & keep your chin up there are better days ahead.

Love & Kisses.
Bill

Feb. 18, 1945
France.

Dear Mom,

I guess its about time I got on the ball, and wrote you a letter.

I'm so sleepy I cant hardly stay awake. I don't know why I should be I didn't get up till about 9:00. We had a pretty good breakfast. We had hot cakes.

We spent most of the morning house cleaning. I had to clean up the back house. I did a pretty good job too. We have a pretty good place to live in at the present. The room I'm sleeping in has a fire place & ever thing. I just finished fixing the light socket. so we now have electric lights. We are really setting pretty.

We had a pretty good dinner today. Which consisted of beans, roast beef, gravy, & of course bread & coffee. They have been feeding us some pretty good meals lately.

If you hear any more about Bob H. let me know.

I've received 3 papers so far, for Dec 30, Jan 1, 13. They provide quite a bit of reading material.

I was informed morning that I'm now a T/5, which means I draw 18 bucks more a month.

Have you gotten settled down in the new place yet. You'll have to write & tell me all about it. What bus line are you nearest?

One of the fellows took my picture the other day. I'll try & get a print & send it to you when he gets it developed.

Well I've got a slew of letters to write and cut this one off here.

Well, Mom take care of yourself & don't work to hard. I'll take care of myself & try to get home as soon as posible.

Love & Kisses
Bill.

June, 25, 1945
Mering, Germany.

Dear Betty & all,

I've received quite a number of letters from you lately, but havn't taken the time to answer them. I'm writing this in bed.

I went to the show tonight It was very good, the picture playing was "The Power of The Whistler." It was very dull.

Some of the fellows went out hunting tonight. They got one deer last night. I went out with them Sat. night, but we didn't get any deer. We seen quite a few, but we couldn't shoot straight enough to hit them. We didn't get home till after 12.

Here is what we had for Sunday dinner yesterday. — All the deer we could eat, spuds & gravey, lettue, corn, lemonade, with peaches for dessert. Not so bad was it! We had liver for dinner today. And I still don't like it.

I've been down stairs playing
with lena, she is sure one heck
of a dog. I think I sent you a
picture of her. Speaking of pictures.
In one of the pictures I sent you it
shows me, two other guys standing
in front of a pill box, rather battered
up. Well, I slept in that pill box
one night. In this letter I I send
you the negitives of two pictures
of me taken with a 35 M.M. camera.
they will have to be enlarged when
printed to be any good. They make
a nice picture though as I have one.
I have some more films being
developed.
    Well, its after 10 so I I
better go to sleep. We have fresh
fried eggs for breakfast ever morning

             good nite,
             love & kisses
             Bill

Aug. 21, 1945.
Furth, Germany.

Dear Mom & all,
I got a letter from you
yesterday that came in eight day.
I'm glad that watch go through
that my pride & joy. The man that
used to own that was an oversee at
the Dachau prison camp. And it is
said that he beat several prisoners
to death. The last I seen of him
he was in a PW cage with a couple
thousand German soldiers. He was
very happy about the whole thing
either.
I don't know how you ever
read my writing. I can't hardly
do it my self. But I know what
I'm writing so I have the advantage.

It was sure nice out today.
I spent most of the afternoon down
at the Red Cross Club. The had some
coke in today. I drank three bottles
and ate about a dozen doughnuts.
I also made a trip down to the APo.
to get some air mail envelops. I rode
the streetcar into Bon in Nurmbg. this eve.
to see if I had any mail. I didn't.
Mail hasn't been coming through too
regular with all the troop movement,
every thing going on.
    I bought me a new shaving brush
today for a mark, a half. But I still
cut myself shaving. - I just can't figure
it out.
    There is a good chance that I'll
be back in the states by the first
of the year or sooner. From what I've
been hearing we might be home in
Nov. I sure hope so.

I'm going to try & get my picture taken at a photo shop. Sat. If I do I send you one. This shop does some pretty good work.

Well I haven't much to write about. All I do is eat & sleep.

You can send another package if you want to. It's alright to send stuff in box a lot of fellows get stuff that way.

Love, & Kisses

Bill.

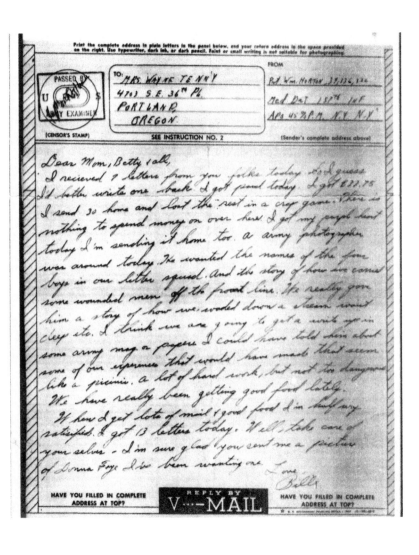

PASSED BY
U _____ S
ARMY EXAMINER
(CENSOR'S STAMP)

TO: MRS. WAYNE TENNY
4703 S.E. 36TH PL.
PORTLAND,
OREGON.

SEE INSTRUCTION NO. 2

FROM
Pfc Wm. HORTON 39,136,***
Med D*t 1ST INF
APO 45 % P.M. N.Y. N.Y.

(Sender's complete address above)

Dear Mom, Betty & all,

I recieved 9 letters from you folks today so I guess I'd better write one back. I got paid today. I got $33.75. I send 30 home and lost the rest in a crap game. There is nothing to spend money on over here. I got my purple heart today I'm sending it home too. A army photographer was around today. He wanted the names of the four boys in our letter squad. And the story of how we carried some wounded men off the front line. We really gave him a story of how we waded down a stream went clear etc. I think we are going to get a write up in some army mag. or papers. I could have told him about some of our experiences that would have made that seem like a picnic. A lot of hard work, but not too dangerous. We have really been getting good food lately.

If how I get lots of mail & good food I'm half way satisfied. I got 13 letters today. Well take care of your selves - I'm sure glad you sent me a picture of Donna Faye I've been wanting one. Love Bill

PURPLE HEART WON BY BILL HORTON

Wounded in action on the Anzio beachhead in Italy, Pvt. William K. (Bill) Horton of Portland, who now has been restored to active duty, has been awarded the purple heart. Prior to receiving his wound, Horton was hero in the rescue of three wounded men.

An army service paper related that Horton was one of three litter bearers who volunteered to go to the aid of five men from another group who had been wounded by mortar shell. The shell made a hit on five GI's wounding them severely. Word of the need for stretcher bearers came back reaching the aid men of Co. F first. They could have passed the job up without anything being said or done; it was clearly a job for the medics of the company to which the injured belonged.

Pvt. John Million, Cleveland, Ten-

Bill Horton

nessee, Pvt. Robert Maxon, Bremington, Washington, and Pvt. William Horton, Portland, Oregon, started on the dangerous trip in the early hours of the evening. It was impossible to make the trip by the direct route; it was necessary to travel by a creek filled with water waist deep.

Two of the men were dead when the medics reached them. The remaining three were loaded on litters, and with the aid of two additional medics from another company, the return trip was started.

The creek was too narrow for two men to walk abrest, so the men worked in relays. They waded a mile through the cold waters of the creek before depositing the wounded men in a collecting station, where they were loaded on an ambulance.

William (Billy) Horton was born and reared in this county and is a grandson of Mr. and Mrs. J. S. Abbott of this city. Billy lived in Jetmore for several years with his mother, the former Mrs. Jessie Hughes until two years ago when the family moved to Portland. He was a junior in high school when they left here.

ACKNOWLEDGEMENTS

The pictures used in this book are either snapshots that were taken by me or of me by my friends, or were taken from two books, both of which were published in 1946. They are *157 th Infantry Regiment – Eager for Duty* and *The Fighting Forty-fifth: A Combat Report of an Infantry Division*. There are pictures of me in these books and I used some of the pictures from these books.

I would like to acknowledge and thank my daughter Kathy Horton-Rose, my granddaughter-in-law Chelsea Heath and my grandson Jonah Rose for all of the hard work and time they put into creating this book. All I did was tell the stories and they did the rest.

-William Horton

Thank you Gramps...

for the laughs

for the stories

for the support

for the wisdom

for the love

for the service

As God spoke to you more than 70 years ago in France during World War II, "I say who and I say when." You were ready for the when, we weren't. I can't wait for everyone to get to read the book and learn about the man, nay, the legend, I was lucky enough to call Gramps.

William Horton
January 6th, 1925 - November 17th, 2018
34,283 days of life lived well.

-Nathan Heath

Living On Borrowed Time

Made in the USA
Middletown, DE
27 July 2022

70084444R00116